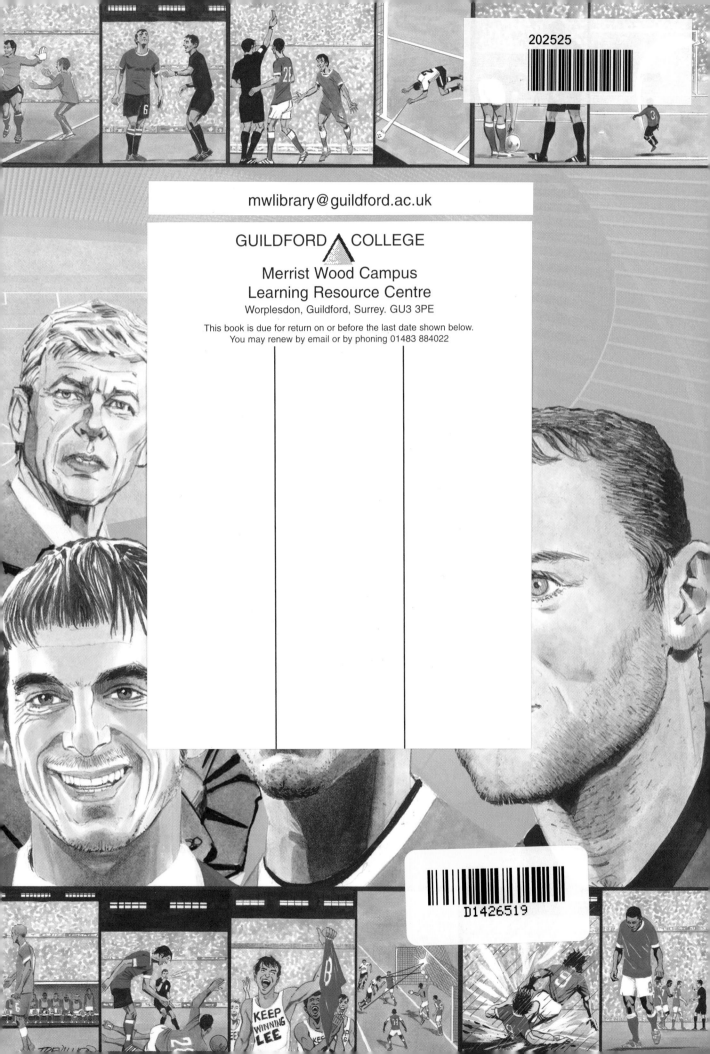

YOU ARE THE REF

3

Paul Trevillion and Keith Hackett

YOU ARE THE REF

3

Over 250 new footballing dilemmas.
Only one answer.
Do you know the score?

First published in 2014 by Guardian Books,
Kings Place, 90 York Way, London N1 9GU
and Faber and Faber Ltd,
Bloomsbury House, 74–77 Great Russell Street,
London WC1B 3DA

2 4 6 8 10 9 7 5 3 1

The photographs on pages 6 and 9 are reproduced courtesy of
the National Football Museum and the Football Association

The statistics used in the infographics on pages 12, 17 and 18
are courtesy of Prozone

A CIP catalogue record for this book is available
from the British Library

ISBN 978-1-783-35021-6

Designed and set by www.carrdesignstudio.com
Editorial Consultant: Justyn Barnes www.justynbarnesmedia.com
Contributors: Mal Davies, David Hills, Steven Bloor
Printed in Italy by L.E.G.O. S.p.A.

Contents

Foreword by Kevin Moore, Director of the
National Football Museum   7

Introduction The Evolution of Football and Its Laws   8

Timeline   10

YOU ARE THE REF: The Dilemmas   20

World Cup Titans

Portugal   24
THE WORLD CUP, RULES AND REFS: A Brief History – 1930-1938 25

Brazil   34
THE WORLD CUP, RULES AND REFS: A Brief History – 1950-1958 35

England   44
THE WORLD CUP, RULES AND REFS: A Brief History – 1962-1966 45

Germany   56
THE WORLD CUP, RULES AND REFS: A Brief History – 1970-1974 57

Argentina   68
THE WORLD CUP, RULES AND REFS: A Brief History – 1978   69

Italy   80
THE WORLD CUP, RULES AND REFS: A Brief History – 1982   81

Netherlands   92
THE WORLD CUP, RULES AND REFS: A Brief History – 1986-1990 93

France   104
THE WORLD CUP, RULES AND REFS: A Brief History – 1994-2002 105

Spain   116
THE WORLD CUP, RULES AND REFS: A Brief History – 2006-2010 117

About the Authors   128

The Secretary - Then suggested that Nos 9 & 10 of the proposed Laws of the Association having been Expunged the Cambridge rules were ~~almost~~ in principle precisely what the association seemed to require - and that it might ~~be~~ be well then to consider whether some of the association should pursue with regard to the Cambridge rules

But it was resolved to proceed with the Settlement of the Laws of the Association; Game; when it was ~~resolved~~ ordered to be as follows:-

1

The maximum length of the ground shall be 200 yards, the maximum breadth shall be 100 yards, the length & breadth shall be marked off with flags; and the goals shall be defined by two upright posts, 8 yards apart, without any tape or bar across them -

2

the winner of the toss shall have the choice of goals. The Game shall be commenced by a place Kick from the centre of the ground by the side losing the toss. the other side shall not approach within 10 yards of the ball until it is Kicked off.

3

After a goal is won the losing side shall Kick off and goals shall be changed

4

A goal shall be won when the ball passes between the goal posts or over the space between the goal posts (at whatever height). not being thrown. Knocked on, or carried.

5

When the ball is in touch the first player who touches it shall throw it from the point on the boundary line where it left the ground, in a direction at right angles with the boundary line

and it shall not be in play until it has touched the ground

6

When a player has Kicked the ball any one of the same side who is nearer to the opponents goal line is out of play and may not touch the ball himself nor in any way whatever prevent any other player from doing so until the Ball has been played: but no player is out of play when the ball is Kicked from behind the goal line.

7

In case the ball goes behind the goal line, if a player on the side to whom the goal belongs first touches the ball, one of his side shall be entitled to a free Kick from the goal line at the point opposite the place where the ball shall be touched - If a player of the opposite side first touches the ball, one of his side shall be entitled to a free Kick (but at the goal only) from a point 15 yards from the goal line opposite the place where the ball is touched. The opposing side shall stand behind their goal line until he has had his Kick.

8

If a player makes a fair catch he shall be entitled to a free Kick, provided he claims it by making a mark with his heel at once; and in order to take such Kick he may go as far back as he pleases, and no player on the opposite side shall advance beyond his mark until he has Kicked

9

No player shall carry the Ball.

10

Neither tripping nor hacking shall be allowed and no player shall use his hands to hold or push his adversary.

11

A player shall not be allowed to throw the ball or pass it to another.

Foreword

I have been a fan of Paul Trevillion's work since my childhood. It's just that for a long time I didn't know it. As a boy, I particularly loved the Roy of the Rovers cartoon strip, but it was only when I became director of the National Football Museum in 1997 that I discovered Paul was the artist whose dynamic style made it so irresistible. I also found that we had a great many other examples of Paul's work in our collection – in comics, magazines, advertising campaigns, and even on the packaging and in the design of football toys and games. Such is Paul's ability and work ethic, I realised that I'd come across his illustrations in many other contexts over the years.

It was therefore a very great pleasure to finally meet him at a special event at the museum in Preston in 2008. Most of the audience present that night, through Roy of the Rovers and the revival of the You Are the Ref strip in the *Observer* in 2006, were also unwitting admirers of Paul's work. As well as regaling us with fascinating anecdotes, Paul did an amazing party piece, turning a drawing of an elephant into Pelé – extraordinary and unforgettable.

The enduring popularity of You Are the Ref, fully six decades after Paul created the concept, is a great tribute to his special ability. The simple idea of readers' questions about refereeing scenarios combined with illustrations grabbed the attention of readers of Tottenham Hotspur's *Lilywhite* magazine in 1952. It soon made its national debut as a strip in the *People* newspaper under the name Hey Ref, also featuring in Roy of the Rovers annuals, before transferring to *Shoot!* magazine in 1969, when the iconic You Are the Ref name was coined. After a couple of substitutions, top-class referee Keith Hackett took up the whistle as arbiter on readers' questions. The combination of Keith's expertise and Paul's powerful drawings – which capture the very essence and spirit of the game – turned the strip into a cult hit. They have been a winning team ever since.

When we were planning to open the new National Football Museum in Manchester, Paul proposed a new interactive game based on You Are the Ref, and this became the centrepiece of our display about the role of the referee. Our team had great fun working with Keith and Paul developing this and it has proved to be a huge hit, enjoyed by more than half a million visitors of all ages and nationalities since the museum opened in July 2012.

As a huge admirer of Paul and Keith's work, it is therefore a great honour for me to introduce this book. I'm sure the numerous dilemmas will test you to the limit of your knowledge of the Laws and, like me, you'll probably get quite a few decisions wrong. And if you too come away with renewed respect for referees and a greater understanding of how difficult their job is, that can only be good for the future of football. More than anything, I'm sure this beautifully illustrated, informative book will enhance your enjoyment of the game we all love.

Kevin Moore
Director
National Football Museum

Above: Kevin Moore holding the historic 1863 Minute Book, containing the minutes from the first meeting of the Football Association and the first official laws of Association Football, handwritten by Ebenezer Cobb Morley

Opposite and on page 9: The Laws of the Game as agreed by the newly formed FA on 8 December 1863

Introduction

The Evolution of Football and Its Laws

Football seems so entrenched in our national culture that it seems hard to believe there was a time without it. Yet the Football Association wasn't formed until as late as 1863. So how did football evolve through the ages until it reached that landmark moment? And how did the referee come to take charge of matches?

Certainly the history of ball games goes back a long way – as early as the sixth century BC in Greece. During the Han Dynasty in China, for 400 years from 206 BC to AD 220, there was Tsu Chu (or 'kick ball'), a popular game that culminated in an annual kickabout on the Imperial birthday. The Japanese evolved a ball game known as 'kemari'. And the Romans invented 'harpastum', played between two teams on a rectangular pitch and introduced to Britain following the Roman invasion.

Ball games continued to be enjoyed in Britain during the Middle Ages, although the definition of what constituted a ball varied widely. The grimmest interpretation came in 1326, when the head of a servant, John de Boddeworth, murdered by two brothers, was used in Cheshire (there were a lot of headers in that match . . .).

The games didn't always meet with official approval. Generations of British royalty, from the English King Edward II to James I of Scotland, criticised men for wasting their time fighting over a ball. Edward III banned football in 1349 because archery practice needed for battle was being neglected for the purpose of 'useless and unlawful games'. By the 15th century, Henry IV went so far as to impose a 20-shilling fine on mayors of towns allowing ball games, while James I banned 'fute-ball' in Scotland, fining offenders 'fiftie schillings'.

But despite this opposition, men still wanted to play football.

The first inkling of professionalism came in 1425 when the prior of Bicester, Oxfordshire, paid players an appearance fee of one groat (4d). Then, a century later, the cause of football was advanced by Richard Mulcaster, headmaster of St Paul's School in London. In 1561, he wrote a treatise claiming that the game provided positive educational values, promoted health and increased physical strength. He also suggested some improvements, such as appointing a trainer and referee.

It would be a while before we would recognise the modern game, though. In its formative years, football was basically a contest played by an anarchic mob without any rules, and involvement meant a high risk of injury, broken legs or even death. Men grabbed the ball and scored, by fair means or foul. A game on Christmas Day, 1719, was recalled by Anna Beynon in a letter. She described how two parishes, Llandysul and Llanwenog, gathered in Bargoed, Ceredigion, West Wales. Following a refreshments break around midday for bread, cheese and beer, men were so drunk that legs were broken and the match became, literally, murderous. Anna, apparently, helped pull a drunken friend away before he was killed.

Luckily other fixtures were more civilised. Football was played at Cambridge University from 1620 and rules were laid down for inter-college matches. Harrow and Eton schools were also at the forefront of the development of the game, from the early 19th century onwards. However, other public schools created their own rules, so that when schoolboys went to university, they discovered they were all used to different regulations, which was rather confusing. So in 1848, there was a meeting at Trinity College, Cambridge, between 14 men from Eton, Harrow, Rugby, Winchester and the 'non-public' schools, to agree on a set of universal football rules. These were subsequently updated in 1854, 1858 and 1862.

Meanwhile the world's first football club, Sheffield, formed by ex-Harrovians on 24 October 1857, was spearheading the development of the game further north. The club established its own set of rules on

> **KEITH SAYS:**
> 'I have had the pleasure of refereeing the historic Sheffield v Hallam derby fixture on a number of occasions. One Christmas, I was on a bus taking me to the game when it crashed on ice. I ended up thumbing a lift and getting to the ground at Dronfield just in time!'

12.

No player shall take the ball from the ground with his hands while it is in play under any pretence whatever.

13.

No player shall wear projecting nails, iron plates, or gutta percha on the soles or heels of his boots.

Definition of Terms

A **Place Kick** - is a kick at the ball while it is on the ground, in any position in which the Kicker may choose to place it.

A **Free Kick** is the privilege of Kicking at the Ball, without obstruction, in such manner as the Kicker may think fit.

A **Fair Catch** - is when the Ball is caught, after it has touched the person of an adversary or has been Kicked or Knocked on by an adversary, and before it has touched the ground or one of the side catching it; but if the Ball is Kicked from behind the goal line, a fair catch cannot be made.

Hacking - is Kicking an adversary intentionally.

Tripping - is throwing an adversary by the use of the legs.

Knocking on - is when a player strikes or propels the ball with his hands or arms.

Holding - includes the obstruction of a player by the hand or any part of the arm below the elbow.

Touch - is that part of the field, on either side of the ground, which is beyond the line of flags.

---

21 October 1858. Penned by Nathaniel Creswick and William Prest, the co-founders of the club, the Sheffield Rules introduced a number of innovations, including the crossbar, corner-kick and throw-in. In 1860, the pioneering club staged the world's first-ever derby match – Sheffield v Hallam. The match was played on the oldest football ground in the world, Sandygate Road in the City of Sheffield.

With so many variations in the rules across Britain, the captains of clubs in and around London felt there was a need to unify them. So on 26 October 1863, they met at the Freemasons' Tavern in Covent Garden, London, and formed the Football Association, with the intention of formulating a set of universal rules for the game of football. At this first meeting, a draft document was drawn up, based on the Cambridge Rules. This was modified and expanded over five subsequent meetings. The FA's appointed secretary, Ebenezer Cobb Morley, was given a week to collate a final set, and eventually, on 8 December 1863, a framework of 13 rules was accepted by the members.

Interestingly, although some attending those early meetings wanted the game to involve kicking and dribbling, others, like representatives of the Blackheath club, wanted tripping, hacking and carrying the ball to be allowed. Ultimately, Blackheath withdrew in favour of developing rugby football.

So when did the referee come in?

Despite its anarchic – and sometimes barbaric – origins, association football was designed to be played by gentlemen. For a short while, the two captains would agree if there was a breach of the rules. Players were expected to own up if they transgressed.

To avoid captains having to come to an agreement, each club supplied its own umpire, both of whom were on the field of play. Players had to appeal to the umpires, stating the offence, before the umpires could give a decision.

If the two umpires disagreed, they would refer the incident to an independent person, a 'referee', for a final decision. The referee wasn't on the field of play; indeed, he was often to be found in the nearest bar, having a drink! Like a high judge in a court of law, all he had to do was listen to both arguments and give his decision.

It wasn't until 1891 that the referee took charge of matches from the middle, and the two umpires – who were still supplied by the opposing clubs – went to the touchlines and became linesmen.

Mal Davies

Timeline

1863

THE LAWS

On 8 December 1863, a set of 13 rules was approved at a meeting of the newly formed Football Association. A month later, the new rules were trialled in a game, which was 14-a-side to accommodate all those interested.

TO HACK OR NOT TO HACK? THAT IS THE QUESTION . . .

The 13 rules adopted by the Football Association and its members in 1863 outlined a game very different, and rather more violent, from football as we know it today.

The field of play was a massive 200 yards by 100 yards, marked by four corner flag posts (there were no other pitch markings) and 'when the ball is in touch the first person who touches it shall kick or throw it from the point on the boundary line where it left the ground, in a direction at right angles with the boundary line'. The loser of the toss kicked off, and opposing players had to be at least 10 yards away. Ends were changed after each goal.

The goalposts were eight yards apart. There was no tape or crossbar and a goal was scored when the ball passed over the space between the goalposts (at whatever height), not being thrown, knocked on, or carried.

A player was 'out of play' (offside) if he was in front of the ball and he had to return behind the ball as soon as possible. A player was allowed to run with the ball towards his opponents' goal if he made a fair catch or caught the ball 'on the first bound'. A fair catch was catching the ball after it had been kicked, knocked on, thrown or had touched an opponent. If the player, after a fair catch, appealed by making a mark at once with his heel in the ground, he was then not allowed to run with the ball.

Neither tripping nor hacking was allowed, and no player could use his hands or elbows to hold or push an opponent, except when a player was running with the ball towards the opposing goal. Then the attacker could be charged, held, tripped, hacked (kicked in the shins) or have the ball wrested from him, but no player could be held and hacked at the same time. Considering all the hacking going on, it is comforting to note that wearing projecting nails, iron plates or gutta-percha (a natural latex) on the soles or heels of boots was outlawed.

1866

OFFSIDE!

A new law was introduced permitting forward passes as long as three defending players were between the receiver and the goal. The goal-kick was also introduced, while the 'fair catch' seen in other codes was eliminated.

TOUCHDOWN!

The first London v Sheffield game took place on Saturday 31 March 1866, at Battersea Park. Rules that differed only slightly from the FA rules were used. It was played in tough conditions and lasted 90 minutes with no half-time interval. Although some of the London team got badly kicked and knocked about, they won by two goals and four 'touchdowns' to nil. A touchdown was when an attacker first touched the ball after it had gone over the opponents' goalline.

London declined a return game, as they only wanted to play under FA rules, and touchdowns were scrapped by the FA in 1867.

1867

ROUGE EXPERIMENT

The Youdan Cup, the first-ever football tournament, was played in Sheffield under Sheffield Rules. The competition was sponsored by a local theatre owner, Thomas Youdan, and 12 Sheffield clubs took part. Three teams contested the final, playing each other in turn at Bramall Lane on 5 March 1867 in front of 3,000 spectators. A four-yard-wide goal was employed, but teams could also score 'rouges' (when a shot at goal would have gone in had the goal been eight yards wide) – the number of rouges was only considered in the event of a drawn game. For the record, the mighty Hallam beat Norfolk and Mackenzie to finish first.

1870

HANDY CHANGES

The specific position of 'goalkeeper' was introduced – he was allowed to handle the ball anywhere on the pitch, but not allowed to carry the ball. Handling the ball became an offence for all other players, and the following year, free-kicks were introduced for handball.

When the ball went over the boundary line, the last person to touch the ball was allowed to restart the game with a one-handed throw at right angles to the boundary line. And if no goals were scored in the first half, the teams would change ends.

1871

UP FOR THE CUP

In October 1871, Charles William Alcock created the FA Challenge Cup, the oldest cup competition. The first FA Challenge Cup final was played at Kennington Oval in March the following year, with Wanderers beating the Royal Engineers 1-0. Mr A Stair of Upton Park had the honour of being the first cup final ref, with umpires JH Giffard (Civil Service) for the Engineers and J Kirkpatrick (Civil Service) for Wanderers.

1872

FOOTBALL GOES INTERNATIONAL

The first international match, between Scotland and England (0-0), was played on 30 November 1872 at Hamilton Crescent, Partick, Glasgow.

FA–SHEFFIELD MASH-UP

The FA was keen to have one set of rules for association football. On 2 March 1872, another Sheffield v London match was played, this time at Bramall Lane. Sheffield Rules were applied in the first half, FA rules in the second – consequently, at half-time the crossbar was lowered from 9 feet to 8 feet. Sheffield edged the cross-code encounter, 2-1.

1873

SCOT'S NEW?

The Scottish FA was founded on 13 March 1873, at Dewar's Hotel, Glasgow.

1874

THE EARLIEST BATH

The FA authorised referees to send players off for certain offences. And now, umpires were mentioned in official FA laws for the first time; previously, disputes were settled by opposing captains.

1875

ICH BIN EIN FUSSBALLER

Oxford University toured Germany, and a number of German universities they visited subsequently took up the game. Germany became one of the first countries outside Britain to play under FA rules.

CORNERED

Corner-kicks were introduced, to be taken from within one yard of the corner flagpost.

1876

WALLY WITH A BROLLY

An umpire used an umbrella during a Scottish Cup quarter-final between Vale of Leven and Queen's Park on 30 December 1876.

WALES KICK OFF

The FA of Wales was founded on 2 February 1876, at the Wynnstay Arms Hotel, Wrexham.

1877

UNIFICATION

In April 1877, the FA and Sheffield football club reached a negotiated compromise. The FA conceded a crossbar (not tape), the corner-kick, and an indirect free-kick for handling the ball. Sheffield accepted three defenders (not two) for offside, throw-ins rather than kick-ins, a goal 8 feet high (not 9 feet), and 11 players on a team.

The length of the game was set at 90 minutes.

1878

BASTARD BLOWS

An Upton Park player, Segar Bastard, became the first referee ever to use a whistle in a game, on 21 December 1878, during the FA Cup second-round match between Nottingham Forest and Sheffield. Mr Bastard blew an 'Acme City' brass whistle, invented by Joseph Hudson in Birmingham around 1875. Hudson's local club, Aston Villa, had refused to allow the new referee's pea whistle to be tested.

Before the whistle, match officials waved a handkerchief, a stick or used their voice.

LET THERE BE LIGHT

On 14 October 1878, the first game using floodlights was played at Bramall Lane, Sheffield, between 'The Reds' and 'The Blues' (0-2), players from local clubs. It was to demonstrate a new form of electric lighting for industrialists. Portable engines behind each goal drove two Siemens dynamos, one for each light.

1880-81

AND HERE COME THE IRISH . . .

The Irish FA was founded on 18 November 1880 at the Queens Hotel, Belfast.

REF RECOGNITION

The 'referee' was mentioned in the laws for the first time. The wearing of shinguards, which had been introduced in 1874, was made compulsory – players initially wore them outside their socks. Touchlines and goallines also appeared in the 1880s.

1882

A raft of new laws came in. For example, playing the ball a second time from a free-kick (and other instances) resulted in a free-kick to the opponents. A player taking the throw-in was required to use both hands (previously throw-ins were one-handed) and could now throw in any direction. It was also made law that the ball must be kicked forward at kick-off.

1885

GOING PRO

The FA 'legalised' professionalism and football soon became the livelihood for some players. As winning became all-important, many players would stop their opponents scoring by fair means or foul, knowing that a goal could not be scored directly from a free-kick.

1886

GIVING THE REF STICK

The FA issued its first memorandum on the guidance of match officials. If an appeal was made by a player and one umpire allowed it by holding up a stick, the referee, if he agreed with him, should instantly sound his whistle without waiting for the opinion of the other umpire.

THE IFAB FORMED

All four British FAs had begun to meet regularly. In offices at Holborn Viaduct, London, on Wednesday 2 June 1886, the International Football Association Board (IFAB) was founded.

The IFAB became the guardian of the Laws of the Game, and the body responsible for any amendments to those laws. They needed to ensure football worldwide was played under the same rules that had been agreed in Britain.

1887

HALF MEASURE

A goalkeeper was restricted to only handling the ball in his own half.

1888

LEAGUE FORMED

The Football League was formed. When the league season kicked off, club umpires operated on the field of play, with the referee off the field.

1891

THE PENALTY-KICK

The penalty-kick was introduced this year. The IFAB approved the Irish FA's proposal, ruling that 'if a defender intentionally trips or holds an opponent, or deliberately handles the ball, within 12 yards of his goalline, the referee shall, upon appeal, award a penalty-kick'.

The kick could be taken from any point 12 yards from the goalline. The other outfield players had to stand at least 6 yards from the ball, and the goalkeeper was allowed to advance no more than 6 yards from his goalline.

Average per Game				
Tackles	31.4	30.2	29.2	30.4
Fouls	12.6	11.5	10.4	10.8
Free-Kicks	15.3	14.3	13.0	13.4
Season	**2009-10**	**2010-11**	**2011-12**	**2012-13**

TECHNICAL TRENDS SINCE 2009-10
Tackles: virtually no change over recent seasons.
Fouls & Free-kicks: small decline since 2009-10; 1.7 fewer fouls per team per match means 3.4 fewer fouls per match in total.
Yellow Cards: virtually no change over recent seasons.

YELLOW CARDS average per Game	
2009-10	1.68
2010-11	1.67
2011-12	1.58
2012-13	1.59

*Figures relate to Premier League only

The first penalty in the Football League was scored by John Heath for Wolverhampton Wanderers in their 5-0 win at home to Accrington Stanley on Monday 14 September 1891.

THERE'S A REF ON THE PITCH . . .

Penalties, of course, had to be awarded by someone, so a referee was introduced to the field of play for the first time. From this point on, a single person with the power to give penalties and free-kicks, without listening to appeals, became a permanent fixture in the game, and the two former umpires became linesmen.

The referee was empowered to caution any player guilty of ungentlemanly behaviour, and, if repeated, send the player off. He could also send off any player guilty of violent conduct. The linesmen's duties were to indicate when the ball was out of play and which side was entitled to a goal-kick, corner-kick or throw-in. They carried a stick (later a flag) to do so, and they were given 'stick' by opposing fans as they were not neutral.

BACK OF THE NET!

Goal nets were introduced this year, too. Everton supporter John Alexander Brodie had his patent for nets approved in November 1890. He had suggested they be used in football after seeing a near riot when a goal was disallowed at Goodison Park in 1889. The FA eventually agreed, and nets were first used in the 1891 FA Cup final, after which they became compulsory for the 1891-92 Football League season.

CENTRE GROUND

A new specification stated that 'the centre of the ground shall be indicated by a suitable mark and a circle radius 10 yards shall be made around it'.

1892-93

LINES AND CIRCLES

Semi-circles with a radius of six yards from each goalpost were drawn on the field of play. The 'penalty line' was drawn across the width of the pitch, 12 yards from the goalline, along which penalties could be taken.

Goalkeepers were also given a little more protection by the ruling that they 'shall not be charged except if he be in the act of playing the ball or is obstructing an opponent'.

REFS UNITED Pt 1

The FA formed the first referees' society in 1893 at Anderton's Hotel, London. Its purpose was to examine the qualifications of referees and to appoint them for matches.

1894

NEUTRAL LINESMEN

It became mandatory for match linesmen to be unconnected to either of the opposing teams.

1895-96

PICKFORD FILES

FA vice president William Pickford was instrumental in producing the first 'Referees' Chart', a booklet which became known as the Laws of Association Football, but is now called the Laws of the Game.

NO RIGHT OF APPEAL

From 1896, appeals by players to referees were no longer allowed. Up to this point, it wasn't unusual for spectators to appeal, too!

1897

11 v 11

It was specified in law for the first time that teams should consist of 11 players and the duration of the game should be 90 minutes unless otherwise mutually agreed upon.

Meanwhile, 'carrying' by a goalkeeper was defined as taking more than two steps whilst holding the ball or bouncing it on the hand.

The dimensions of the field of play were also specified in law – length: 100-130 yards; width: 50-100 yards. The length had to exceed the breadth.

1898

THE FOUR-MONTH MATCH

On 26 November, a First Division game between Sheffield Wednesday and Aston Villa was abandoned in the 79th minute, with Wednesday leading 3-1. The remaining minutes of the match were played four months later, during which Wednesday scored another goal to run out 4-1 winners.

At the time, the league's rules stated that in the event of an abandoned game, the teams must return at a later date to play out the remaining time. Aston Villa appealed against travelling all the way to Sheffield to play 10 minutes in a probable lost cause. Their appeal was unsuccessful, but the upshot of the farce was that all future abandoned English games had to be replayed in their entirety.

Not the case in Spain though, where, 97 years later, in June 1995, the Copa del Rey final between Deportivo La Coruña and Valencia had to be abandoned, also in the 79th minute, due to a waterlogged pitch at the Santiago Bernabéu stadium. The score was poised at 1-1, and when the last 11 minutes were played three days later, Alfredo scored the winning goal for Deportivo to claim the trophy.

1901

BAGSY GOALIE!
Teams were required to nominate a goalkeeper and inform the referee if the goalkeeper was changed.

1902

AREA CODE
The penalty area (18 x 44 yards) and goal area (6 yards x 20 yards) were introduced to the pitch. A 12-yard penalty mark replaced the 12-yard penalty line and it was made compulsory to mark out a halfway line across the field of play.

1903

GOALS DIRECT
The 'direct free-kick' was added to the Laws. From then on, a goal could be scored directly from a free-kick awarded for a foul on an opponent or for intentionally handling the ball.

PLAY ON!
The new 'advantage' clause allowed referees to wave play on for the first time.

1904

FIFA FOUNDED
The Fédération Internationale de Football Association (FIFA) was founded on 21 May 1904. It was important that the FA joined to ensure that the Laws as laid down by the IFAB were followed. The FA and associations from seven other countries joined within two years, and Englishman Daniel Burley Woolfall (1906-18) became the second president.

> **KEITH SAYS:**
> 'I proudly served on FIFA's Referees' Panel from 1981 to 1991.'

1905

DROP IT
The 'dropped ball' was introduced. Back in 1888, the ref would throw it up instead.

1907

CORNERS DIRECT
It was made legal for a goal to be scored directly from a corner-kick. The offside law was also updated, so a player could not be deemed 'out of play' (offside) if he was within his own half at the moment the ball was played by a teammate.

1908

REFS UNITED Pt 2
The Referees' Union was formed on 9 May 1908.

1913

STAY IN THE BOX
It was ruled that goalkeepers could only handle the ball inside their penalty area.

TEN PACES
At a free-kick, the offending team had to remain at least 10 yards from the ball until the ball was played (previously, it was 6 yards).

FIFA BECOME IFAB-ULOUS
FIFA joined the IFAB. Initially, the four British associations had two votes each, while Baron de Laveleye (Belgium) and Mr CAW Hirschman (Netherlands) of FIFA had a vote each.

1914

GENTLY DOES IT . . .
At dropped ball, referees were instructed to drop the ball and not throw it down hard on the ground.

1920

THROW ONSIDE
The law was amended so a player could not be offside from a throw-in.

1921

REFS UNITED Pt 3
The Referees' Union is renamed 'The Referees' Association'.

1925

THREE BECOMES TWO
Some defenders had mastered the 'offside trap', resulting in too many free-kicks for offside, so the law was changed. From then on, two defenders (which was the number originally cited in the Sheffield Rules) had to be between the opponents' goalline and the attacking player instead of three.

On the first day of the 1925-26 season, Aston Villa beat Burnley 10-0 as the Burnley defenders struggled to come to terms with the new law.

1929

WALK THE LINE
The law was changed, requiring goalkeepers to stand on their goalline until the ball was kicked at a penalty-kick.

In other news, a player with faulty boots was allowed to rejoin the game once they were mended; previously, he had remained off the field of play.

1931

FOUL PUNISHMENT

If it was a foul throw, the throw-in went to the opponents. Previously, the punishment was a free-kick.

1936

KICK IT OUT!

Lifting the ball up from a goal-kick into the goalkeeper's hands was banned – the ball had to be kicked out of the penalty area to be in play. A similar rule was brought in the following year for free-kicks to the defending team in the penalty area.

1937

NO ENTRY TO THE ARC

The penalty arc – the D-shape at the edge of the penalty area – was introduced to ensure all players other than the taker were at least 10 yards (9.15 metres) away from the ball and to prevent defending players impeding the kicker's run-up.

BETWEEN THE STICKS

Another amendment to the penalty laws required the goalkeeper to stand between the posts. Previously, some goalkeepers (especially at the very sporting Corinthian club) had stood outside the goalposts and made no effort to save the ball, reasoning that if their team gave away a penalty then their opponents were entitled to score!

HEAVIER BALL

The standard weight range of the ball was increased slightly from 13-15 oz to 14-16 oz.

1938

ROUS-ING DEVELOPMENTS

The format of the Laws was changed and renumbered by Stanley Rous, then-secretary of the FA, later appointed CBE in 1943, knighted in 1949 and elected the sixth president of FIFA (1961-74).

1948

STAY OUTSIDE

Opposing players were made to stand outside the penalty area for a goal-kick. Previously, they only had to remain a minimum of 10 yards from the ball.

1949

SEVEN OR MORE

A law was introduced stating that: 'A match shall not be considered valid if there are less than seven players in either team.' Many years later, on 16 March 2002, referee Eddie Wolstenholme abandoned a game between Sheffield United and West Bromwich Albion after 82 minutes, because the Blades had only six

players left – three had been sent off and two were off injured. West Brom were leading 3-0 at the time . . .

1958

RIGHTS TO VOTE

New voting rights were determined by the IFAB, with each British association reduced to having one vote instead of two, FIFA having four, and any proposal needing at least six votes in favour. This voting split remains the same to this day.

BRING ON A SUB

Substitutes were introduced.

KEITH SAYS: 'I commenced my refereeing career in 1960, officiating my first game at Cadman Road between Hillsborough Boys Club and Sheffield United Juniors.'

1961

LAW WOE

The 1898 law change requiring a full replay of abandoned matches came back to haunt Denis Law in a January FA Cup tie between Luton and Manchester City. When the game was called off with 20 minutes remaining, City were leading 6-2 and lethal Law had scored all six. Sadly for him, all six goals were expunged from the record books. Even worse, when the game was replayed a few days later, Luton won 3-1 (Law scored City's only goal).

1967

FOUR STEPS AND RELEASE

Goalkeepers were now required to release the ball after four steps. The law stated: 'the keeper must not take more than four steps whilst holding, bouncing or throwing the ball in the air and catching it again without releasing it so that it is played by another player.'

1968

SPIT AND GO

'Spitting at opponents, officials or other persons, or similar unseemly behaviour' was deemed to be violent conduct and a sending-off offence.

1970

LIGHTBULB MOMENT

Yellow and red cards were introduced to communicate a caution and sending-off. Former referee Ken Aston came up with the idea whilst sitting in his car at a set of traffic lights.

1980

SPITTING DIRECT AND INDIRECT

Spitting at an opponent while the ball is in play was made a penal offence, punishable by a direct free-kick. The sanction for spitting at match officials or other persons, or similar unseemly behaviour, remained an indirect free-kick.

1984

INDIRECT MOVE

Indirect free-kicks awarded to the attacking team a couple of yards from the goalline were proving almost impossible for referees to police, as the defenders on the goalline were so close to the ball. The law was thus amended so the kick would be taken 'from that part of the goal area line which runs parallel to the goalline, at the point nearest to where the offence was committed'.

1986

HAPPY HUNDREDTH

IFAB celebrated their 100th anniversary in Mexico City, and Mexico also hosted the World Cup.

1987

ADDING TIME

The law was amended to compel referees to allow for time lost through 'substitution, the transport from the field of injured players, or time-wasting'. Previously, referees were allowed to use their discretion for these three circumstances when considering how much time to add on at the end of a match.

FOUL THROW

A throw-in taken from the wrong place became a foul throw, and a throw was awarded to the opposing team. This was introduced to discourage the players on a winning (or drawing team) from taking throw-ins from the wrong place to waste time, knowing that the ref would just order a retake.

1988

MIND ME SHINS, PLEASE

Wearing shinguards was made compulsory

1991

AND THEN THERE WERE FOUR . . .

The fourth official was introduced.

DOG & DOGSO

A red card became mandatory for denying an obvious goalscoring opportunity (DOGSO) or an obvious goal (DOG) by deliberately handling the ball on the goalline.

1992

NO GOING BACK

The back-pass rule was introduced, disallowing goalkeepers from picking up a ball passed back to them by a member of their own team. The punishment for doing so was an indirect free-kick from wherever the goalkeeper picked the ball up. This has proved an excellent rule, creating a much quicker game.

1993

IN THE ZONE

The 'technical area' was introduced: any coaching must be done from within its confines.

1995

EXTRA SUB

Three substitutes were now allowed in matches instead of two.

NO MORE INTENT

The word 'intent' was removed from the Laws. Six of the ten penal offences were classified as 'careless' (no card), 'reckless' (yellow card) or 'using excessive force' (red card). 'Intentionally obstructing' was no longer in the Laws – it became impeding.

OFFSIDE . . . OR NOT?

The offside law was changed to account for 'active' and 'inactive' players.

1996

REFS' HELPERS

'Linesmen' (and female 'lineswomen'/female 'linespersons') were given the new title of 'assistant referee'.

1997

FRESH START

The captain who won the toss used to have the choice of either which goal to attack or to kick off, but few captains chose to kick off anyway, so this was revised to simply having a choice of ends. The ball was deemed to be in play 'once it is kicked and moves', simplifying the over-fussy old rule that it had to travel the 'distance of its circumference'. Scoring a goal directly from kick-off also became legal – previously another player had to touch the ball.

CH-CH-CHANGES

It was a vintage year for law amendments. Other changes included the prohibition of the goalkeeper picking the ball up directly from a throw-in (as with a back-pass), the term 'ungentlemanly conduct' replaced in the Laws by 'unsporting behaviour', and

Total Distance (m)

*Figures apply to Premier League only

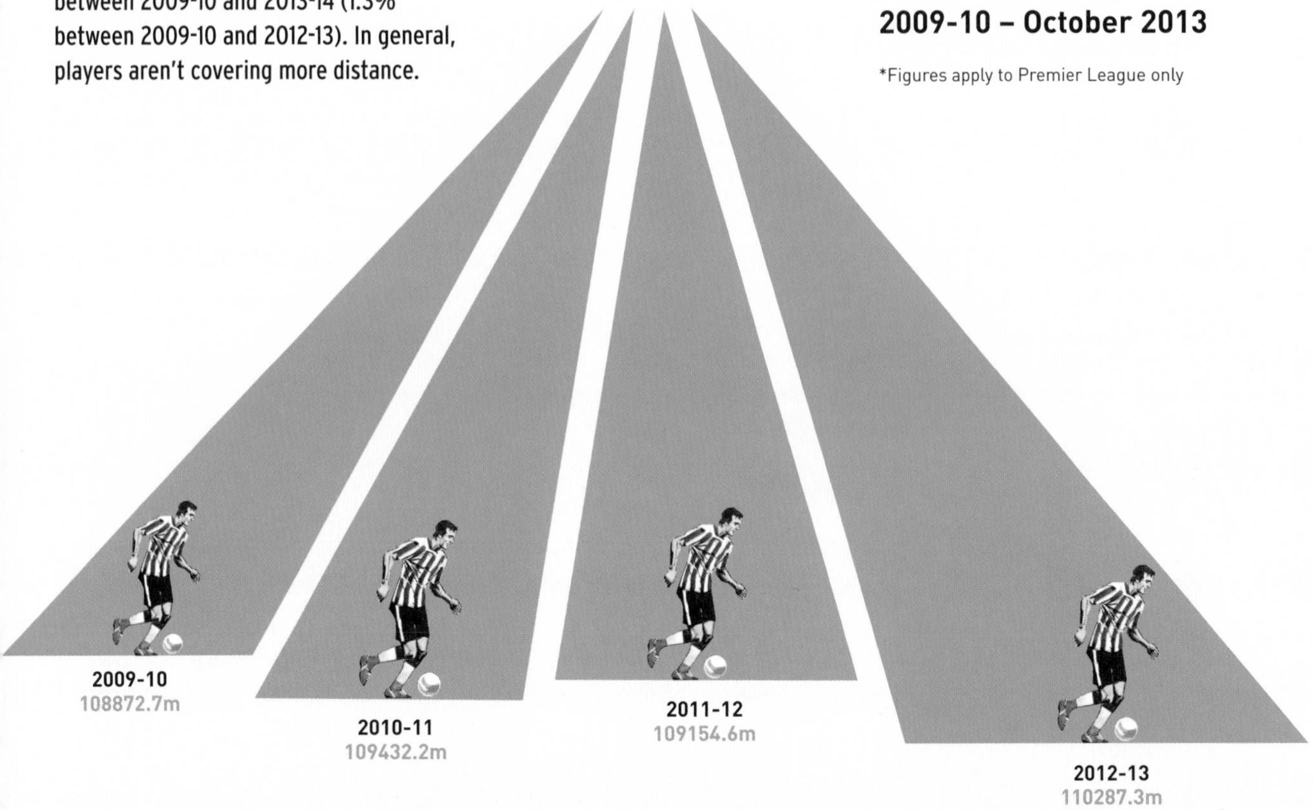

PHYSICAL TRENDS SINCE 2009-10

Total Distance: only a 0.5% increase between 2009-10 and 2013-14 (1.3% between 2009-10 and 2012-13). In general, players aren't covering more distance.

2009-10
108872.7m

2010-11
109432.2m

2011-12
109154.6m

2012-13
110287.3m

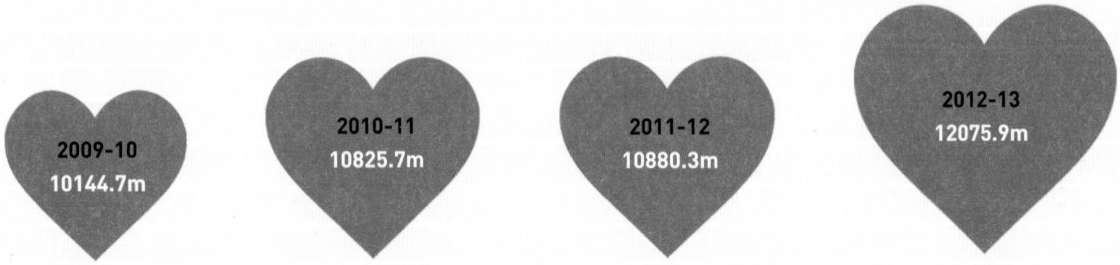

2009-10
10144.7m

2010-11
10825.7m

2011-12
10880.3m

2012-13
12075.9m

High-intensity Distance: teams ran 19% further at high-intensity speeds in 2012-13 compared to 2009-10, an increase of 1.9km across the team.

High-intensity Time: teams spent 18% more time at high-intensity speeds (> 5.5m/s) in 2012-13 compared to 2009-10, an increase of over 4.5 minutes across the team.

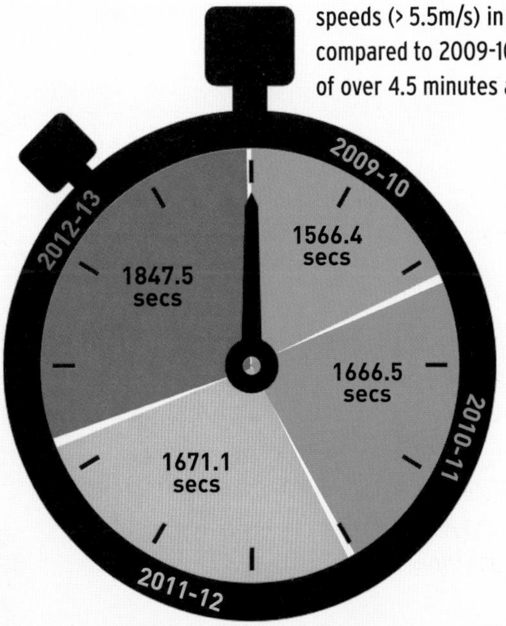

2009-10
1566.4 secs

2012-13
1847.5 secs

2010-11
1666.5 secs

2011-12
1671.1 secs

Pass Success %: increased 4.5% from 2009-10 to present. This reflects an increased technical competency in the Premier League as well as a move towards ball-retention tactics.

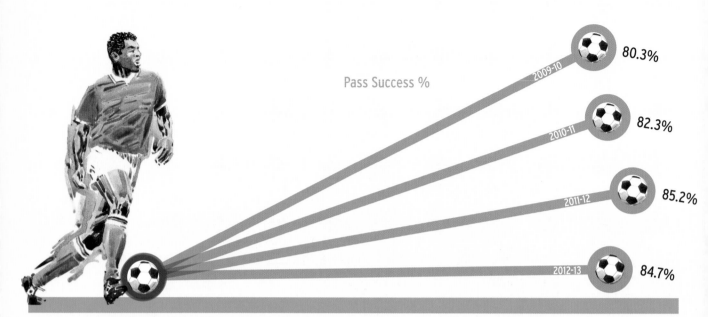

Pass Success %

2009-10 — 80.3%
2010-11 — 82.3%
2011-12 — 85.2%
2012-13 — 84.7%

UNLUCKY SEVENS

In 1997, seven red-card and seven yellow-card offences were categorised:

YELLOW CARD OFFENCES (CAUTIONS)

- Unsporting behaviour
- Dissent by word or action
- Persistent infringement of the Laws of the Game
- Delaying the restart of play
- Failure to respect the required distance when play is restarted with a corner kick, free-kick or throw-in
- Entering or re-entering the field of play without the referee's permission
- Deliberately leaving the pitch without the referee's permission

RED CARD OFFENCES

- Serious foul play
- Violent conduct
- Spitting at an opponent or any other person
- Denying the opposing team a goal or an obvious goalscoring opportunity by deliberately handling the ball (this does not apply to a goalkeeper within his own penalty area)
- Denying an obvious goalscoring opportunity to an opponent moving towards the player's goal by an offence punishable by a free-kick or a penalty kick
- Using offensive, insulting or abusive language and/or gestures
- Receiving a second caution (yellow card) in the same match

'offensive, insulting or abusive language' replacing 'foul or abusive language'. Oh, and it was stipulated that if thermal undershorts were worn, they must be of the same main colour as the team's shorts.

1998

DANGER! Pt 1

A revised law stated that 'a tackle from behind that endangers the safety of an opponent must be sanctioned as serious foul play', and would be punishable by a red card.

HURRY, GOALIE!

A goalkeeper was deemed to be 'time-wasting if he holds the ball in his hands or arms for more than 5-6 seconds' (the time limit was set more precisely at six seconds in 2002).

KEEP YOUR SHIRT ON

Referees were instructed to caution players for removing their shirt in celebration of a goal.

2005

NEW OFFSIDE
IFAB decided to clarify offside with a New Offside Interpretation (NOI), but in the 2005 FIFA Confederations Cup, FIFA issued its own interpretation of the NOI. An emergency meeting of the IFAB was held in August, and FIFA had to withdraw its interpretation.

NO BLING
Jewellery, and taping to cover jewellery, was no longer allowed.

2-METRE RULE
At a throw-in, 'all opponents must stand no less than 2 metres from the point at which the throw-in is taken'.

DANGER! Pt 2
A small, but significant, change to the law on dangerous tackling was made. The words 'from behind' were removed to read: 'A tackle that endangers the safety of an opponent must be sanctioned as serious foul play.'

2006

GET OFF!
A law amendment required that 'a player, substitute or substituted player who has been sent off and shown the red card must leave the vicinity of the field of play and the technical area'.

2008

GOALLINE ASSISTANCE
IFAB authorises UEFA to experiment with two extra assistant referees, one behind each goalline.

2009

STAY IN PLAY
For the purposes of offside, any defending player leaving the field of play for any reason without the referee's permission was considered to be on his own goalline or touchline until the next stoppage in play. The ref was now empowered to caution any defender who left the field of play deliberately to place an opponent offside.

2010

WHEN TO FEINT
A law was passed saying that while feinting in the run-up to take a penalty in order to confuse the goalie is allowed, feinting to kick the ball once the run-up is complete is unsporting and a yellow-card offence. This was introduced because some players stopped, waited for the goalkeeper to dive one way, and then scored on the other side of the goal.

2011

OBJECTIVE CHANGE
Referees were mandated to stop the match if 'an extra ball, other object or animal enters the field of play . . . only if it interferes with play', restarting the game with a dropped ball. This clarification was prompted by Darren Bent's goal for Sunderland against Liverpool (1-0) in October 2009. Bent's shot deflected in off a beach ball thrown onto the field by a Liverpool fan who was behind the goal.

2012

HAND BOOKED
A player deliberately handling the ball to prevent an opponent gaining possession became a yellow-card offence.

NO MORE 'DROPPED GOALS'
The dropped-ball law was changed to state that if a dropped ball is kicked directly into the opponents' goal, a goal-kick is awarded; if it is kicked into the team's own goal, a corner-kick is awarded to the opposing team. This was to avoid a recurrence of a situation like the 2004 Carling Cup tie between Yeovil and Plymouth Argyle. Yeovil's Lee Johnson scored as his pass back from a dropped ball caught the Plymouth goalkeeper off his line. Yeovil manager Gary Johnson (Lee's father) sportingly told his team to allow Plymouth to score from the kick-off. Steve Crawford ran through unchallenged, to make it 1-1. Yeovil won 3-2 in extra time, with Lee scoring a hat-trick that included the goal from the dropped ball.

2013

OFFSIDE UPDATE
The offside laws were tweaked to clarify the situation with regard to 'interfering with an opponent', and 'gaining an advantage' from 'rebounds and deflections'.

COME IN NUMBER FIVE AND SIX . . .
Additional assistant referees – the fifth and sixth officials – were introduced.

GLT
The principles, requirements and specification of Goal-Line Technology (GLT) were enshrined in law for the first time. Happily, this radical move came 47 years too late for Geoff Hurst's goal to be disallowed!

Mal Davies

You Are the Ref: The Dilemmas

ANSWERS

1) The defenders are right: the smoke does represent an outside agent. You should have stopped play the moment the ball entered the cloud but either way, the decision is the same: the game restarts with a drop ball on the six-yard line parallel to the goalline.

2) Cool the situation down with firm, clear communication. First, ask the physio to treat the injured forward, who must leave the field after treatment. Second, take the physio aside and spell out some home truths: he must not enter the field of play until he receives a signal to do so from you, his observations on what he claims to have seen on TV are irrelevant, and, in any case, the law forbids the use of TV equipment in the technical area. Third, take the necessary action against the offender (red, yellow or no card at all), and, finally, after making sure the TV equipment is removed, restart with a direct free-kick. After the game, report everything that happened to the appropriate authorities.

3) If you are unsure whether the ball crossed the line on the first phase of this incident, you cannot award the goal. Instead, work on the basis that it did not – so restart with a direct free-kick to the defence, and show the striker a yellow card if you feel the handball was deliberate.

▲▲ A high ball lofted into the box briefly disappears into a cloud of smoke pouring from a canister thrown by a fan. When the ball hits the ground, a striker pokes it into the net. Defenders are furious: they want you to disallow the goal for 'outside interference'. What now?

▲▲ A forward who is famous for his theatrical overreactions goes down under a heavy challenge. As you run over to assess him the player's physio suddenly races on to the pitch, screaming that he just saw a TV replay in the dugout and it was a definite red card offence. There's uproar. What do you do?

▲▲ A defender blasts a clearance right off the line. As the attacking side appeal for a goal, claiming that the ball had gone in, the clearance hits a striker's outstretched hand and flies back into the net. Hawk-Eye registers the ball going in – but you don't know whether that was for the original shot or the handball rebound. Do you award the goal?

▲▲ A striker scores from what looks like an offside position, but your assistant fails to flag. He points out that a defender off the field, behind the goalline receiving treatment for an injury, had both legs still on the field of play. What now?

▲▲ A defender reacts to a striker taking a tumble in the box – which you ruled a fair challenge – by trying to pull him to his feet. But the striker resists angrily, convinced he has been fouled. The tug of war results in the defender falling, landing awkwardly and crying out in pain. What do you do?

▲▲ In a non-league game the home goalkeeper is wearing a very baggy jersey – and manages to pull off a save using a flap of material running from his elbow to his waist. Opponents howl. What now?

ANSWERS

1) Disallow the goal. The defender was naive in not leaving the field completely, and you were wrong not to make sure he was completely off the pitch – but that does not change the fact that he is inactive. You gave him permission to leave the field, he is not part of the game, so he is not playing the striker onside.

2) Award a penalty. The original challenge may have been fair, but once the striker resists the defender's help, the defender is guilty of holding his opponent. That is punishable by a penalty and a yellow card for unsporting behaviour. The fact that the defender was hurt in the incident does not change how you should deal with it.

3) Goalkeeper shirts do have additional protective padding in them, but anything out of the ordinary needs to be checked with you before kick-off. Had he done so you would have stopped him wearing it: adding 'wings' like this is an illegal modification, and effectively an extension of his arms. So stop play, show him a yellow card for unsporting behaviour and restart with an indirect free-kick on the goal area line.

1) Stop play. Anything that might constitute either an attempt to gain an unfair advantage or a possible health and safety risk needs to be dealt with swiftly. Ask the player to join you at the technical area with his manager, and try to establish what the substance is, and whether it can be removed. Do not allow him to return to the pitch until you are satisfied that the smell is no longer an issue – and if he cannot remove it, he has to be substituted. Restart the game in the usual way, having made it clear that you are going to report the matter to the authorities.

2) You cannot show two red cards. The goalkeeper was not guilty of denying an obvious goalscoring opportunity because the ball ran to another striker who had a clear shot at goal. So show the keeper a yellow card for his foul, send off the defender, and restart with a penalty-kick. This is another scenario that shows how quickly referees need to be able to think under pressure.

3) Whether it is intentional or not, the penalty taker has played the ball twice – so disallow the goal and restart with an indirect free-kick to the defending team from the penalty mark.

▲▲ Soon after a sub comes on, opponents start complaining that he is giving off a foul, rotten egg smell. They are right. You suspect he may have deliberately broken a stink bomb to keep defenders away from him. The sub denies everything. What now?

▲▲ A keeper commits a professional foul as a striker is about to score, but, seeing the ball run to another forward, you play advantage. But before the forward can tap the ball into the net a chasing defender sends him flying – another professional foul, again denying an obvious goal-scoring opportunity. What do you do?

▲▲ As a player takes a penalty his standing foot accidentally touches and slightly moves the ball, a split second before his other foot smashes it into the net. The keeper protests. Goal or no goal?

▲▲ A player goes down injured, and the only sub available to replace him is his player-manager – who you sent to the stands earlier in the game for abusive behaviour. What now?

▶▶ The home team are winning 5-0 on a foggy autumn evening. On 88 minutes the fog suddenly becomes so thick it is impossible to continue. Do you blow for full-time, or abandon?

TREVILLION-

▲▲ A penalty smashes against the post, rebounds, hits your assistant without going out of play and then deflects back to the taker – who slots it into the net. How does play restart?

ANSWERS

1) When you dispatched the player-manager to the stands, you should have done so with a red card, making clear he was being dismissed in both his capacity as a manager and as a substitute. He cannot take any further part in the game in any capacity.

2) Stop the game and approach the ground controller and stadium manager, advising them that you are taking the players off and suspending the game temporarily. They will in turn advise the crowd that you are going to wait and see if the fog lifts to allow the match to finish (which has happened for me in the past). But if the fog sits where it is, abandon the game and report what happened to the authorities. It is up to them to either order a replay or let the score stand.

3) It's not a goal: the taker has committed an offence by playing the ball a second time without it being touched by an opponent. So restart with an indirect free-kick to the defending team from where the offence occurred.

PORTUGAL

World Cup winners	-	
World Cup runners-up	-	
Third place	1	(1966)
Fourth place	1	(2006)
World Cup hosts	-	

Eusebio

The 'Black Pearl' made his mark on World Cup history by becoming the top-scorer, with nine goals, in the 1966 tournament. Six of the nine were scored at Goodison Park, including four goals in the quarter-final against North Korea to power his team's recovery from a 0-3 deficit to win 5-3.

TREVILLION

THE WORLD CUP, RULES AND REFS
A BRIEF HISTORY – 1930-1938

1930

MEDIC KOs HIMSELF!

During the semi-final between USA (a team consisting largely of ex-Scottish and English pros) and Argentina, USA's physio ran onto the pitch to make a complaint to the referee. He was so animated he accidentally broke a bottle of chloroform in his medical kit, was promptly overcome by the fumes and had to be stretchered off.

> The first goal in a World Cup finals game was scored by Lucien Laurent of France on 13 July 1930 in a 4-1 win over Mexico.

SHARP-DRESSING JEAN SEEKS QUICK GETAWAY

Belgian referee Jean Langenus took charge of the first-ever World Cup final, between Uruguay and Argentina, a tense repeat of the 1928 Olympic final which Uruguay had won 2-1. Langenus only agreed to officiate a few hours before kick-off – he wanted a boat ready for him one hour after the final whistle in case he had to make a quick getaway!

Pre-match controversy over the choice of match ball was resolved when it was agreed that Argentina would use their ball in the first half and Uruguay theirs in the second.

> The first hat-trick was scored by Bert Patenaude for USA against Paraguay (3-0).

> Italy hosted the 1934 finals tournament, but still had to qualify – the only time the hosts were not given automatic qualification.

> The group stages of 1930 were discarded in favour of a straight knockout competition in 1934 and 1938.

Some 93,000 people turned up to watch at the Centenario Stadium, Montevideo, on 30 July and Langenus came on to the pitch resplendent in a suit jacket, golfing plus-fours and a natty red-striped tie.

Argentina used their ball to build a 2-1 half-time lead, but the host nation's team scored three with their ball after the interval to win 4-2 and become champions of the world.

1934 & 1938

HAIL IVAN, GEORGE . . . AND FRANKENSTEIN!

Nothing of any great note to report on the reffing front . . . unless you're related to Ivan Eklind (Sweden) or Georges Capdeville (France), who had the honour of refereeing the 1934 and 1938 World Cup final matches respectively.

It's also worth remembering that Hungary's 4-1 win over Bulgaria in a World Cup qualifier on 29 April 1934 was refereed by one Hans Frankenstein. Scary!

> Peru's Plácido Galindo earned infamy as the first player to be sent off in a World Cup finals fixture, against Romania.

1) Award the goal. You and your assistants are part of the game, and if the ball hits any one of you, play continues. In this case, the flag is considered an extension of your assistant's arm. You must, though, have a word with your colleague about his positioning: clearly this should never have happened.

2) The striker is in an obvious goalscoring position, so your instinct must be to play advantage and await the outcome. If he scores – with the correct ball – award the goal, then show the defender a yellow card for unsporting behaviour. If the striker fails to score, allow play to continue and caution the defender at the next stoppage. For the record, had the striker been inside the box but not in an obvious goalscoring position, you would have stopped the game, awarded a penalty for attempting to strike an opponent, and shown the defender a red card.

3) Stand by your decision, and remind them, firmly, of their obligations. Advise both managers that if they delay sending their teams out beyond the standard 15-minute break then their clubs are likely to face significant sanctions, on top of the individual punishments they have already earned. If one or both continue to refuse to allow their team to play, you may be forced to abandon the game.

▲▲ A ball which is about to bounce over the touchline hits your assistant's flag and stays in play. A winger runs onto it, whips in a cross and a striker nods it home. What now?

▲▲ Seeing a striker burst through on goal, a desperate opponent tries to put him off by blasting a spare ball at him. The keeper reacts by stepping out of goal, both arms in the air, appealing for you to stop play. What do you do?

▲▲ After a furious half-time bust-up you send both managers to the stands. They are outraged, and refuse to send their teams out for the second half unless you reverse your decision. What now?

▲▲ A team celebrate a stunning late winner by removing their shirts to reveal messages of support for their manager's sick son. Five of them have already been booked – and the opposition demand you dismiss them and abandon the game. What now?

▲▲ In a Sunday morning game, a fierce shot smashes the underside of the crossbar and knocks it clean off. Before the bar hits the ground, a striker heads the rebound into the net. Do you award the goal?

▲▲ You take an accidental tumble and, by the time you are upright again, the ball is in the net. You have no idea how it got there – and, as one team celebrate, the other insist you missed a foul in the build-up. Your assistants are split: one thinks it was a fair goal, the other disagrees. What now?

ANSWERS

1) Due to the sensitive nature of the celebration you can use your discretion here, and avoid turning this into a farce: allow the game to come to its conclusion, and report the incident to the authorities afterwards.

2) Disallow the goal. The Laws of the Game state that the goal must have posts and a crossbar – so as soon as you saw the bar become dislodged you should have blown the whistle. As it is, make it clear that the goal does not count, and explain why. Make sure that the bar is replaced, safely, before restarting with a dropped ball on the six-yard line parallel to the goalline, at a point nearest to where the ball made contact with the bar. If it cannot be replaced safely, abandon the game.

3) While I would never want to rule out a valid goal, this is a difficult situation. You did not see the crucial passage of play – and, while normally when a referee is unsighted like this he can opt to base his decision on the views of his colleagues, when there is clear disagreement between them, a goal cannot be fairly awarded. So you have no option but to rule it out, and restart with a dropped ball from where it was when you were knocked over.

ANSWERS

1) The Laws only cover celebrations by players, stating that referees are 'expected to act in a preventative manner and to exercise common sense in dealing with the celebration of a goal'. So, as long as it is not excessive, allow the subs to celebrate. If they have delayed the restart, though, caution one or two of the worst offenders. As for the goalscorer: his celebration does not merit a second yellow card.

2) This legal corner tactic was used early on in the Portugal group game against the Netherlands in Euro 2012. Nani tapped the ball forward, Meireles ran over, intending to dribble the ball towards goal and catch the defence unaware. But Sneijder was aware of the ploy. When Meireles saw him, he placed the ball back in the quadrant. The assistant should have flagged for deliberate handball – a direct free-kick to the Netherlands. Luckily, Portugal did not score from the corner.

3) It's a goal. In law, a player can now only be said to be gaining an advantage if he plays a ball that rebounds to him off a goalpost or the crossbar or an opponent. The scorer did not play the ball off a rebound, and the defence should not have left him unmarked.

▲▲ A player on a yellow card smashes in a stunning goal and races over to the touchline to celebrate – where the subs spill on to the pitch as they embrace him. What do you do?

▲▲ You spot a player trying to take a sneaky 'hidden' quick corner, nonchalantly nudging the ball forward for a teammate to dribble it towards goal. But a defender also spots them and runs over, so the teammate instead picks the ball up and places it again, ready to take a 'normal' corner. Do you intervene?

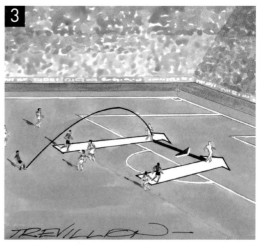

▲▲ A midfielder lobs a ball over the defence for a striker to run onto. The striker, running from an outside position, controls the ball and lays it off to a colleague – who was clearly in an offside position when the lob was played. But he was behind the ball when it was crossed to him, and he fires it into the net. What do you do?

28

1

▲▲ A defender, desperately trying to kill time by holding the ball in the corner, uses the flagpost as leverage to maintain his balance. His opponents complain and stop challenging him. What do you do?

2

▲▲ The away team's nippy wingers have destroyed the home defence in the first half. To try to disrupt them, the home manager orders his groundstaff to repaint the touchlines at half-time, making the pitch narrower but still within legal dimensions. Do you intervene?

3

▲▲ It's a penalty shoot-out at the end of a cup final. An extraordinary 21 penalties have been taken and scored – but the final player is young and inexperienced. Overawed by the occasion, he refuses to take a penalty, and wants his side's star man to take it instead. What now?

ANSWERS

1) Stop play. Players cannot use the flagposts to keep themselves upright – and they should know that. Show the defender a yellow card for unsporting behaviour and restart with an indirect free-kick.

2) Yes, and quickly. You need to stop this happening. If the lines are already redrawn, have the new markings removed and the old ones restored. In the professional game, clubs have to register the size of the field of play before the start of the season and they are not then allowed to change it during the season. In any case, playing conditions in the first and second half must be the same.

3) Speak to his captain and ask him to persuade the youngster to take his kick. This is a big problem: the Laws require him to take the kick and you cannot continue unless he does so. If he still refuses, show him a yellow card for unsporting behaviour and if that makes no difference, abandon the tie. It's a nightmare scenario all round but you have no option. Report everything that happened, including the details of all your conversations, to the appropriate authorities after the game. They might decide to award the cup to the opposition, rather than have the whole final replayed.

ANSWERS

1) There's no need here to worry about deliberate handball or the denial of an obvious goalscoring opportunity, because play was not live. The ball needs to leave the penalty area before it is in play from a goal-kick. So calm everyone down, and award a retake of the goal-kick.

2) You might not be happy, but you do not outrank the police. If they deemed it so serious that they had to make an immediate arrest – despite the risk of crowd provocation – then you have no power to intervene. Stop play, inform the players' managers that you will allow the handcuffed player's team to make a substitution as you have not shown a red card, and restart with a dropped ball. Report everything that happened to the authorities.

3) There have been cases when referees have shown empathy to a player removing a shirt to pay tribute to a deceased loved one – but that's not the case here. You are in the job to apply the Laws fairly and consistently, not to pick and choose them. So, while it's hardly going to make you popular, you need to show this player a second yellow, then a red. He shouldn't be too upset: he knows the Laws and, in any case, he doesn't need to worry about suspension: this is the final minute of his final game. He'll always be remembered as the player who scored a goal and never played again.

▲▲ A keeper scuffs a goal-kick, which dribbles across the penalty area. A defender, spotting a striker racing in, panics, throws himself forwards and grabs the ball. What do you do?

▲▲ Two players clash off the pitch. Neither you nor your assistants saw it – but two nearby police officers wade in. You're stunned to see them then handcuff one of the players. What now?

▲▲ A local hero on his much-hyped final appearance for his boyhood club scores a stunning last-minute winner. Overjoyed, he tears off his shirt and throws it to the crowd. He has already been booked. What now?

1

▲▲ A player slips while taking a throw-in. As he falls he releases the ball: it's an obvious foul throw, but the ball lands at the feet of an opposition striker who has a clear run on goal. Do you play advantage?

2

▲▲ A player with a reputation for diving goes flying in an attempt to win a penalty. But before you blow your whistle, intending to book him for simulation, he pokes out a toe and knocks the ball into the net. What now?

3

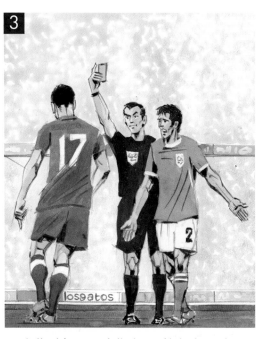

▲▲ In the dying seconds the home side try to run down the clock with a substitution. The subbed player walks off deliberately slowly, and fails to respond to you urging him to hurry up, so you book him. But that still makes no difference. What now?

ANSWERS

1) Playing advantage whenever possible is definitely good practice, but that is not an option here. The foul throw happened as a result of him slipping before the ball left his hands, which made it an incorrectly taken throw-in. So stop play and order a retaken throw-in.

2) You cannot allow a player to benefit from cheating – and if he hadn't taken the dramatic leap he would not have been in the position to nudge the ball into the net. So disallow the goal, caution the forward for unsporting behaviour, and restart with an indirect free-kick to the defending team.

3) Cheating does not get more obvious than this. Show him a second yellow, followed by a red. And the substitution is cancelled: it is not complete until the player leaving the pitch has stepped over the touchline, and the player joining the game has entered the field of play. If the team still want to make a change, then they need to pick a new outfield player to take off.

ANSWERS

1) If he was unhappy with the position of the ball, he should have asked to adjust it before taking the kick. He has no right to complain now. My advice to officials in these situations is always to let the player take the appropriate action to keep the ball still, to avoid such accusations.

2) No goal. Really the goalkeeper should have been a bit braver and stood his ground, but either way this counts as interference from an outside agent. Disallow the goal and restart with a dropped ball on the goal area line that is parallel to the goalline at a point nearest to where the ball entered the goal. Make sure the eagle is coaxed to safety, and report the facts after the game.

3) The Law is quite clear on this: 'A player must be cautioned if he removes his shirt or covers his head with his shirt.' Players know they will pick up a yellow card for celebrating in this way, but they still carry on doing it – clubs just do not seem to take sufficient action against players who might be suspended for a game after picking up five yellows. So what do you do here? Caution all of them: 11 yellow cards. The club will be fined for exceeding five cautions in one game, which will hopefully inspire them to take some proper disciplinary action.

▲▲ In high wind, the ball will not stay still on the penalty spot – so you use your heel to make a dent. A striker takes the kick and scuffs it wide – then angrily demands a retake. He says the dent you made was too deep. What now?

▲▲ Just after kick-off, an eagle – part of the home club's pre-match entertainment – breaks away from its trainer and lands on the away team's crossbar. Their goalkeeper, terrified of birds, runs away – and is immediately beaten by a quick-thinking striker, before you stop play. Goal or no goal?

▲▲ The home side score late on and the whole team simultaneously take off their shirts and wave them round their heads in celebration. Do you book the scorer, the captain, the whole team, or no one at all?

▲▲ After a controversial penalty decision, the whole away team bench – manager, assistants, subs and physio – spring to their feet and scream foul verbal abuse at you. What now?

▲▲ The home keeper, who has made three world-class saves, keeps taking long sniffs from his towel. At half-time, the opposition manager alleges the keeper is inhaling a banned stimulant. What action do you take?

▲▲ The ball is running out of play, and you're not sure who touched it last. But before you need to decide, an over-enthusiastic ballboy, who has been told not to waste time, dashes on and passes the ball straight to the keeper. What now?

ANSWERS

1) This sort of situation does untold damage to football's image, and you need to deal with it firmly. Identify, if possible, the main offenders and then deal with them as follows. First, show a red card to any guilty substitute or substituted player. Second, if the manager or his coaches are guilty, dismiss them from the technical area to the stands. Third, if the physio was involved, make a note: he or she needs to remain available, but you would include them on the list of dismissals in your post-match report. Restart with the penalty.

2) You cannot possibly intervene at this stage – the keeper may have a perfectly good explanation, and you're hardly equipped to work out exactly what it is that he is sniffing. After the game, though, make sure the towel is bagged and handed over to doping officials for inspection, and include the incident in your report.

3) Stop the game and award a dropped ball from where the boy touched it. You don't need to stop play if a ballboy (or any other outside agent) enters the field of play, but you do if he, she or it has a direct impact on play, as in this case. You should have a word with the boy, and include what happened in your report.

BRAZIL

World Cup winners	5	(1958, 1962, 1970, 1994, 2002)
World Cup runners-up	2	(1950, 1998)
Third place	2	(1938, 1978)
Fourth Place	1	(1974)
World Cup hosts	1	(1950)

TREVILLION

Pelé

Pelé became the youngest-ever player to compete in a World Cup final at the age of 17 years and 249 days, scoring two goals in a 5-2 win over Sweden, and he would grace three more World Cup finals. He was named player of the tournament in 1970 as Brazil triumphed again – they beat Italy 4-1 in the final, with Pelé scoring the opening goal. Oddly, England fans' most enduring memories of Pelé in that tournament are of him being denied as a result of a miraculous reflex save by the great Gordon Banks and a perfectly timed tackle by Bobby Moore in Brazil's 1-0 group match win over the defending champions.

To Paul
Good luck
Pelé

TACTICS AND TECHNIQUES

1950

ENGLAND SHAME, READER'S PRIDE

The first World Cup after the Second World War was played in Brazil. Referees were saved a potential injury-fest when FIFA refused India permission to play barefoot and the Indians promptly withdrew from the tournament. Shamefaced England stars probably wished they had withdrawn after suffering an embarrassing 1-0 defeat by USA (Generoso Dattilo of Italy reffed the match, trivia fans).

One Englishman who could hold his head high was referee George Reader, chosen to officiate at

> England, Scotland, Northern Ireland and Wales all qualified for the 1958 tournament in Sweden, the first and only time all four home nations have qualified for the World Cup finals.

the final, a 2-1 win for Uruguay over hosts Brazil. Reader was watched by a record-smashing crowd of 199,954 at the Maracana stadium in Rio.

No pressure, then . . .

Reader, who was a spritely 53 years old when he took charge of the final, remains the oldest-ever referee of a World Cup match. One of his linesmen was Arthur Ellis, who later earned fame as the referee in TV game show *It's a Knockout*.

1954

AMATEUR GLORY

To celebrate the 50th anniversary of FIFA, the finals were held in Switzerland, where the organisation is based. For the second tournament in succession, an Englishman refereed the final – William Ling. West Germany won the match 3-2 against Hungary at the Wankdorf Stadium, Berne, to become champions, a remarkable achievement as Germany's team were amateurs – there was no professional league in the country at that time.

1958

GOALLESS FOR MAURICE

The 1958 finals in Sweden were notable for the feat of ace French striker, Just Fontaine, who scored 13 goals, a tournament record. Seventeen-year-old prodigy Pelé scored six goals in four matches, notching two in Brazil's 5-2 final win over the host nation, and finishing tied for second in the goalscoring chart. Pele hadn't played until the last of Brazil's group matches, missing a 0-0 draw with England. Refereed by Maurice Guigue of France, it was the first-ever goalless match in World Cup finals history.

1) A terrific question – it just illustrates how you need to be prepared for anything, and for decisions which involve several elements. First, dismiss the goalkeeper for denying an obvious goalscoring opportunity. Second, dismiss the defender for using excessive force in violently ripping the shirt. Once the defending team have a new goalkeeper in place – either an outfield player or a sub – restart with a penalty-kick.

2) No. The Laws allow for a goalkeeper to wear tracksuit bottoms but not outfield players, who should be wearing shorts. If they really insist, I would let them play in tights, providing they are the same main colour as the shorts.

3) There are two offences here, and they happened almost simultaneously: the keeper handling a back-pass, and the striker dispossessing him. If you follow the letter of the law, you should respond to simultaneous offences with a dropped ball, but in practice it is far better to be decisive and rule which offence came first. I would say that the handling of the back-pass was the first infringement, as it was the back-pass itself that led to the incident. So disallow the goal and restart with an indirect free-kick to the attacking side. You should, though, also caution the striker for endangering an opponent.

▲▲ A striker racing in on goal has his shirt pulled so violently that it rips clean off, leaving him in just his club-coloured vest. But he stays upright and tries to round the keeper – who brings him down just as he goes to shoot. The ball runs out of play. What now?

▲▲ On a bitterly cold day, the home captain informs you his side, already wearing gloves, have decided to play the second half in tracksuit bottoms. They are the same colour as their shorts. Do you let them?

▲▲ A striker races onto a back-pass, prompting the keeper to leap forward and place both hands on top of the rolling ball. As he does so, the striker toe-pokes it out of his possession into the net. What now?

1

2

▲▲ A winger reacts to being tripped by rolling theatrically - an attempt to get his opponent booked. The angry defender reacts by gently nudging him with his foot, rolling the winger over the touchline into a pile of snow. The winger leaps up and hurls a snowball at the defender, which hits you in the face by mistake. What now?

▲▲ Before a penalty shoot-out you spot one of the teams inserting contact lenses. They turn out to be opaque, intended to stop the keeper seeing where they are looking. Should you intervene?

3

▲▲ A striker in the box shouts 'near post' to a player about to chip in a cross. The call distracts his marker, who instinctively moves towards the near post. But the striker hesitates, reads the flight of the ball, backs off and, unmarked, heads it into the net. What now?

ANSWERS

1) Dry your face, ignore the laughter and call both players to you. First, the defender. He is guilty of unsporting behaviour in rolling the winger off the pitch, but he did not use excessive force – so it is a yellow card for him. Second, the winger. He's guilty of attempting to strike an opponent, which leaves you with no option: send him off, and restart with a direct free-kick for the initial trip.

2) No. In the time available, you cannot judge what effect these lenses will have. Your instinct may be that it represents unsporting behaviour, but really this is an issue to be dealt with by the authorities after the game. Provided they have not delayed the taking of the kicks, allow the shoot-out to continue.

3) Allow the goal. The defender should react to what he is seeing, not to what is being shouted. If the attacking player had shouted 'Leave it!' or 'My ball!' then I would have disallowed the goal and cautioned the forward for deceiving an opponent, which represents unsporting behaviour. As it is, this is the sort of shout that happens plenty of times in a game: defenders need to be alert.

ANSWERS

1) As always when there are two offences, punish the first. The law states clearly: 'Feinting in the run-up to take a penalty-kick to confuse opponents is permitted as part of football. However, feinting to kick the ball once the player has completed his run-up is considered an infringement of Law 14 and an act of unsporting behaviour for which the player must be cautioned.' That is what you have to do. The keeper being off his line would only be a consideration once a valid penalty-kick had been taken. Restart with an indirect free-kick to the defending side from the penalty spot.

2) If you're going to show a straight red card you need to be entirely satisfied that you heard and understood what the player said. If you have any doubt, then take him to one side and issue him with a warning. If, though, you judge that his smile and gesture represented dissent, show him a second yellow card, followed by a red.

3) This is down to your ability to interpret events accurately in an instant. If you feel with total confidence that this was a con, that the handball was deliberate, award a penalty and dismiss the player for denying an obvious goal. In my view, you cannot know that for sure. Restart with a corner-kick.

▲▲ A penalty-taker ends his run-up with a brief tactical pause just before smashing the ball into the net – rattling it past the keeper, who had clearly come off his line before the kick was taken. What is your decision?

▲▲ You book a French player for a foul. He responds by shaking his head, smiling and making a remark to you in his native tongue. A French opponent runs over and says it was a grossly offensive insult – and, with your limited smattering of GCSE French, you are inclined to agree. What action do you take?

▶▶ As a defender sprints back to stop the ball trickling into the empty net, he appears to tear his hamstring. As he falls forwards, he knocks the ball wide of the goal with his hand. What do you do?

1

▲▲ A defender goes in with a high challenge but you play advantage, intending to caution him at the next stoppage. The attacking move continues and, a few seconds later, the same defender commits a handball. What do you do now?

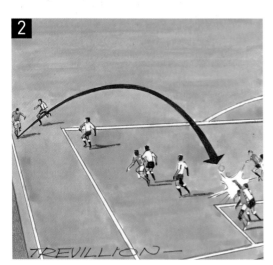

2

3

▲▲ As a long ball is clipped forward into the area, you spot a striker trying to run back into an onside position – only for his marker to block him, deliberately keeping him offside. Before you react, the striker breaks free and converts the chance. Does the goal stand?

▶▶ It's a crucial final-day relegation six-pointer. In the second half you notice that the visitors' goalkeeper has a mobile phone sitting behind the goalline and is using it to check the scores from other games while the ball is upfield. What now?

ANSWERS

1) The defender has committed two cautionable offences: the fact that you played advantage does not change that. Stop play, show him two yellow cards and then a red. If possible in this situation, though, you should try to warn the defender he will be cautioned after you have played advantage: that might have made him think twice about committing the second offence. Preventative refereeing is always a good policy.

2) No goal. As always, punish the first offence. The defender has not physically manhandled the striker into an offside position: the striker was already in an offside position before the defender blocked him. So declare him offside when he plays the ball, immediately speak to both players to calm the situation – again, trying to prevent trouble – and restart with an indirect free-kick.

3) At the next stoppage, deal with this as unsporting behaviour and caution (book) the keeper. Electronic communication between coaches and players is banned and I would deal with this as a breach of those regulations. Arrange for the mobile phone to be removed.

ANSWERS

1) If the keeper had only made contact because you were in his way then you would allow play to continue – but as he has used you to gain an unfair advantage, show him a yellow card for unsporting behaviour. Restart with an indirect free-kick from a point on the six-yard line closest to where the offence took place. It cannot be a penalty as the offence was not committed against an opponent. You also need to rethink your positioning and viewing angles: you were too close to play.

2) Challenge him. Ask him for more information, and if you are not satisfied about his impartiality, dispense with his services, use a replacement official and report him to the authorities. Clearly this was not a good appointment: officials are always asked to declare allegiance to any team.

3) At the next stoppage, summon the player and his captain and inform them that, if there is another act of misbehaviour that you consider to demonstrate a lack of respect for the game, you will indeed show him a second yellow card for unsporting behaviour.

tigerm

▲▲ As the ball flies into a crowded penalty area the keeper leaps to punch clear – boosting himself into the air by putting one hand on your shoulder. Attackers appeal for a penalty: they say the keeper denied an obvious goalscoring opportunity by using you to gain an unfair advantage. What now?

▲▲ During the break you spot that one of your assistants, who has flagged for two controversial penalties to the away team in the first half, has a tattoo of the club's crest on his upper arm. What do you do?

▲▲ With his side cruising to victory, a winger, already on a yellow, decides to use the final five minutes to mock media critics who called him a 'diver' pre-match. Every time the ball comes near him, he comically hurls himself to the ground. He is not trying to cheat – but opponents still want him sent off. What do you do?

1

▲▲ As you blow for a direct free-kick to be taken, two players from the attacking side, who are standing by the wall, begin fighting with each other. It totally distracts the opposition – and while they turn to watch, the kick-taker curls the ball into the net. You realise the fight was a ruse. What now?

2

▲▲ One of your assistants alerts you that he is being repeatedly racially abused by a small group in the crowd behind him. What action do you take?

3

▲▲ A striker fires a long-range effort in on goal. The keeper, realising he can't get to the ball, instead hangs off the crossbar, lowering it by an inch and causing the shot to hit the bar rather than go in. What do you do?

ANSWERS

1) It may be a ruse, but it's a half-baked one. Fighting on the field of play is the most obvious form of violent conduct, whether it involves opponents or colleagues. So disallow the goal, show both players a red card, and restart with an indirect free-kick from where the fighting took place.

2) Deal with this in stages. First, using your communication system, ask the fourth official to summon the stadium security officer to the technical area. At the next stoppage, speak to the officer and ask for extra stewarding on that line and for CCTV to be focused on the area. If the problem continues, you have several options, including simply swapping the two assistants over or even abandoning the match. Either way, report everything that happened to the authorities.

3) You need to be certain here that the lowering of the bar definitely prevented a goal. If you are sure, send the keeper off for denying a goal, and restart with an indirect free-kick on the goal area line, parallel to the goalline. If not, show the keeper a yellow and restart in the same way.

1) There is no offence here. The unattached boot may have denied an obvious goalscoring opportunity, but it was a fluke: it was not thrown, so there is no infringement to deal with. The boot did, though, interfere with play like any other 'outside agent', so you need to stop the game and restart with a dropped ball.

2) Yes, you need to act – not over the undignified sacking, but over the use of electronic communication systems between players and staff. Get a message to the new manager requesting him to stop – and reminding him he cannot enter the technical area either, as his name is not on the team sheet. Afterwards, include what happened in your report.

3) The striker has not made contact with the goalkeeper, but he is guilty of an offence. The Laws state: 'The goalkeeper is considered to be in control of the ball by touching it with any part of his hands or arms' – so you need to penalise the striker's challenge. Disallow the goal and restart play with a direct free-kick to the defending team.

▲▲ A striker skips past a fair challenge from the last defender but then trips over the defender's loose boot, which came off in the tackle. Before the striker can recover, the keeper collects the ball. What do you do?

◄◄ The home chairman responds to a first-half fan protest by sacking his manager at half-time and immediately hiring a replacement. The new man then starts directing proceedings by phone from the stands. Do you intervene?

▲▲ A keeper catches a high ball above his head firmly with one hand – only for a leaping striker to head it out of his grip into the net. What do you do?

For a special Christmas edition of You Are the Ref, Sylvester Stallone made a guest appearance . . .

▲▲ It's 1943 and you're in charge as a team of Allied prisoners take on Germany. At half-time you spot four POWs plus all the subs escaping down a tunnel in their dressing room. What action do you take?

▲▲ In a last-gasp melee the ball drops at your feet. Overexcited, you instinctively lash it into the net. As you wheel away to celebrate, what do you do next?

▲▲ A team of strugglers run out for the second half in sponsored Santa hats and branded strap-on beards. They look sad, but their angry chairman says it's all they're good for. What now?

ENGLAND

World Cup winners	1	(1966)
World Cup runners-up	-	
Third place	-	
Fourth place	1	(1990)
World Cup hosts	1	(1966)

Bobby Moore

Named by Pelé as the best defender he ever played against, Moore is the only England captain to hold the World Cup aloft. Ever the gentleman, Moore famously wiped his hands on the velvet tablecloth before shaking the hand of the Queen as she presented him with the Jules Rimet Trophy at Wembley in 1966.

Trevillion

1962

ASTON & THE 'BATTLE OF SANTIAGO'

The World Cup in Chile was marred by violence, and English ref Ken Aston was the unfortunate man in black charged with overseeing the most notorious game, between the hosts and Italy. Among the match's lowlights, Italy's Giorgio Ferrini was sent off by Aston after just 12 minutes (Ferrini refused to leave the pitch and had to be removed by policemen). Chileans Honorino Landa and Leonel Sánchez got away with punching opponents. Sánchez did it twice, breaking Humberto Maschio's nose with a scything left hook. His previous assault on Mario David had prompted David to kick him in the head, an action for which the Italian was dismissed.

1966

CAUTION CONFUSION

Back in the days when there were no yellow and red cards, the referee had to rely on other communication skills to caution and send off players. And sometimes communication broke down, as in England's ill-tempered 1-0 World Cup quarter-final win over Argentina at Wembley.

After 35 minutes, referee Rudolf Kreitlein of West Germany dismissed Argentina's captain, Antonio Rattín. It took almost seven minutes for him to leave the pitch. England's Charlton brothers, Bobby and Jack, were also cautioned in the game for ungentlemanly conduct, but were not aware they had been.

Rattín was given a four-match ban, two other Argentinian players received three-match suspensions for assaults on FIFA officials, and the Argentinian FA were fined a measly $150, the maximum amount at the time.

The long-term consequence was the introduction of red and yellow cards in 1970.

This simple but effective innovation was the brainchild of Englishman Ken Aston, who had been head of FIFA's Referees' Committee at the time of the 1966 World Cup.

THAT 'GOAL'

In the 10th minute of extra time in the final between England and West Germany, Geoff Hurst crashed an Alan Ball cross against the crossbar and down. Swiss referee Gottfried Dienst conferred with Azerbaijani linesman Tofik Bakhramov and awarded a goal.

Enhanced footage has since shown that the ball did not actually cross the line . . . but never mind, eh – we won 4-2!

ANSWERS

1) There is no reason why not: they have asked permission and it does not contravene a law. All you need to be wary of is that there is no unnecessary delay or obvious gamesmanship. When the opposition player is walking up to take his kick, the change of keeper should already be taking place. If done fairly it's an interesting tactic.

2) Show the taker a red card for his rugby tackle, then order a retake. That may seem like an odd call given the taker's action, but the same law applies in a shoot-out as with a normal penalty-kick: 'If the player taking the penalty-kick infringes the Laws of the Game and the ball enters the goal, the kick is retaken.' The retake must be taken by a teammate who has not yet taken a kick.

3) A clear attempt to gain an unfair advantage but you do have to send both players off. Their star player can now take the kick (indeed any of the other players can take it, as the order does not need to be the same). Clearly you would include all the details in your post-match report, so the authorities could consider further action.

▲▲ Before a shoot-out you are surprised when a captain asks if they can put an outfield player in goal for every other kick, alternating with the keeper. He thinks it will put the opposition off. What is your response?

▲▲ The decisive kick in a shoot-out is tipped onto the post and bounces back along the goalline. As the keeper leaps up to stop the ball, you are astonished to see the penalty-taker rugby tackle him. The ball rolls into the net. What now?

▲▲ Another shoot-out is 9-9 after 18 kicks. The home side score the 19th, meaning the away team must not miss theirs. But the two players who've not yet taken a kick suddenly start swearing at you. They clearly want to be sent off, so that their star striker can take the crucial kick instead. What now?

46

▲▲ You award the away team a penalty. As the taker composes himself, the stadium announcer advises the goalkeeper over the PA which way to dive. What now?

▲▲ A defender tries to hook a waist-high ball off the line just as a striker launches a diving header. In order to protect his face the striker blocks the defender's foot with his hand – and heads the ball into the net. Is it a goal?

▲▲ As a striker leaps to head the ball into the net a defender behind him holds him back by putting his hands on his shoulders. But at the same instant, another striker commits an identical offence – levering himself up off the defender's shoulders and powering a header into the net. What now?

ANSWERS

1) You cannot intervene during the game: the kick has to be taken, whatever anyone in the stadium is shouting. Calm everyone down and allow the kick to go ahead, but before restarting the game advise the home team's officials that the incident will be reported, and that they need to make sure there is no repeat.

2) No. The striker might very well have been trying to avoid injury, but whatever his reasons, he is guilty of pushing an opponent. Restart the game with a direct free-kick to the defending team.

3) Strictly, if two opponents commit offences of the same nature simultaneously, you are supposed to stop play, take any necessary disciplinary action (such as a yellow card for unsporting behaviour), and restart with a dropped ball. But in practice, it is better to be decisive and make a judgment: penalise one of the offenders and look confident in doing so. The defender cannot be penalised for denying an obvious goalscoring opportunity as the ball ended up in the net – so penalise the second attacker for holding down the defender in order to score. It's a direct free-kick to the defending side.

ANSWERS

1) This scenario is common enough to have been defined in the Laws of the Game. As the defender has effectively left the field of play to commit the offence, you need to stop play, and restart with an indirect free-kick. And, as this took place adjacent to the goal area (the six-yard box), the kick is taken from a point on the goal area line parallel to the goalline, nearest to where the infringement occurred. Also, you need to caution or send off the defender, depending on the severity of the challenge and whether it denied an obvious goalscoring opportunity.

2) What a daft gesture. If he had removed his shirt in a goal celebration that would be an automatic second yellow – but in this case, although you could regard it as unsporting, I would issue a stern warning instead. And, as the shirt pulling had happened a couple of times before, show the marker a yellow card for unsporting behaviour, then restart with a direct free-kick to the striker's team.

3) You can score directly from a goal-kick – but only into the opponents' net. In this case, as the ball left the penalty area before being blown back, restart with a corner.

▲▲ A winger races into the penalty area along the goalline and tricks his way past a defender. As he does so he briefly steps off the pitch, at which point the defender trips him. The ball stays in play. What do you do?

▲▲ A striker already on a booking has his shirt pulled by his marker, as has happened a couple of times before. Angrily, he takes his shirt off and sarcastically hands it to his opponent. What do you do?

▲▲ In high wind, a goalkeeper takes a weak goal-kick: it balloons up out of the penalty area but is caught by a gust and flies back over his head into his own net. What now?

▲▲ A striker is clipped as he rounds the goalkeeper but he manages to stay on his feet, so you play advantage. But immediately the ball bobbles and he controls it with his hand before firing it into the net. What now?

▲▲ A goalkeeper fumbles a catch, deflecting the ball behind him. As he turns he sees it rolling slowly towards his empty net, so in desperation hurls one of his gloves at it – and successfully diverts it to safety. What now?

◄◄ Before a game you spot that a winger is wearing tiny shinguards with the sides cut away. He insists only the shin bone needs protecting. Do you allow him to play?

ANSWERS

1) You rightly played advantage, and the striker failed to take it. If he had not then gone on to commit an offence you would have taken play back to the original foul and awarded a direct free-kick – but the striker's action negates that. You need to show two yellow cards: the keeper for his foul (unsporting behaviour) and the striker for deliberate handball. Restart with a direct free-kick to the defence.

2) The Laws state that shinguards must be worn, but there is no written regulation on the design. It is simply down to you to decide if the shinguards provide an adequate degree of protection. I would allow the player to play with this minimum form of protection provided it does not create a danger to him or his opponents.

3) It's a clever trick, but not a legal one. Stop play, show the keeper a yellow card for unsporting behaviour and restart with an indirect free-kick to the attacking side on the goal area line parallel to the goalline, nearest to where the ball was when play stopped.

ANSWERS

1) Calm everyone down and, with your colleagues, take control of the situation. Send the manager out of the technical area and call both captains over to you. Explain that, because you cannot award a free-kick against a manager, the game will now restart with a dropped ball. It's an extraordinary scenario, but extraordinary scenarios do happen every season across the country. You need to be ready for anything.

2) It doesn't. This won't be popular, but you are not in a position to modify the Laws of the Game as you go – so you'll have to abandon the match. League organisers will have to think again, and consider using smaller pitches, which are permitted for over-35s.

3) First things first. There are strict rules around the use of mobile phones and other devices by match officials: for good reason, they have to be switched off in the dressing room. But seeing as you have been made aware of what's going on, you do need to deal with it. Allow the game to continue as normal but at the end ask the player, his manager and the club secretary to join you in your dressing room. Inform them that you are aware of the allegations and make clear you will be including them, and any comments they make in response, in your report to the authorities.

1

▲▲ The home side pile forwards looking for a vital late winner – only for the ball to be booted back upfield towards the opposition's unmarked winger. As the winger controls it, you're astonished to see the home manager race on and rugby tackle him to stop him having a clear run on goal. There's an uproar. What now?

2

▲▲ You're refereeing the inaugural match of a new over-70s league. During the game it becomes clear that one of the keepers does not have enough strength in his legs to propel his goal-kicks outside the penalty area. His teammates also fail. How does play restart?

3

▲▲ In the half-time break after a stormy first 45 minutes, your assistant calls you over and points out that the home side's star striker has been using the interval to tweet grossly offensive remarks about you. What do you do?

1

▲▲ The ball runs out of play towards where the subs are warming up. One of them instinctively puts his foot out to trap the ball – and stops it before it has completely crossed the line. What do you do? How does play restart?

▶▶ A Sunday league side have lost their corner flags, so have improvised by taping toilet rolls to the top of each flagpost. The groundsman says it will aid visibility, and will not be a danger to the players. Do you start the game?

TREVILLION

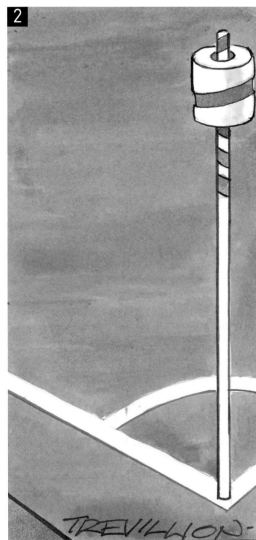

3

▲▲ In the first few minutes a defender trots over to you to complain about the 'distracting' bright-green strapping a winger is wearing round his ankles. He says it is giving his opponent an unfair advantage. What is your response?

ANSWERS

1) Show the substitute a yellow card. It may seem harsh but he has effectively entered the field of play without permission, and you have to apply the Laws consistently. Restart with an indirect free-kick to the opposition, taken from where the ball was when you stopped play.

2) This is one of those questions which proves a referee needs to be ready for anything. The Laws of the Game are clear: flagposts are compulsory, but the actual flags are not. So yes, a game can be started with flag-less flagposts. All you need to be sure of is that whatever is taped to the posts does not represent a danger, and toilet rolls are safe enough. But after the game, include the details in your post-match report. This clearly isn't good for the image of the competition.

3) It's a valid complaint. The law was recently changed on this issue and now stipulates that 'any tape or similar material must be the same colour' as the part of the sock to which it is applied. At the next break in play, ask the player to leave the field to remove or replace the strapping, and make a mental note: you and your colleagues should have spotted this before kick-off.

ANSWERS

1) The opposition's anger is understandable. I would judge this situation based on the severity of the impact: at the very least this is a reckless, yellow-card offence, but if the sub is seriously injured then I would show the winger a red card for excessive force. Sadly for the opposition, adding a replacement sub to their bench is not allowed under the Laws: you need to calm them down and explain that clearly.

2) Yes. A swap like this can be made if it involves an outfield player who was on the field at full-time and in extra time. The manager is not allowed to bring on a substitute unless the goalkeeper is injured and unable to continue.

3) This type of holding, pulling and grappling happens far too often these days: it has to be stopped. The fact that these two players are technically off the field of play is irrelevant – it is an offence and you need to intervene. Disallow the goal, caution the striker for unsporting behaviour and award an indirect free-kick to the defending team. It can be taken from anywhere inside the goal area (the six-yard box).

▲▲ A flamboyant winger races to the corner flag after scoring and launches into his trademark somersault celebration. But he misjudges the flip and collides with an opposition sub, leaving the sub injured. The opposition are outraged and want to add a new sub to their bench. What now?

▲▲ In a penalty shoot-out a manager is disgusted with the way his keeper let in the first three kicks, and wants to swap him with an outfield player who is not one of their five named takers. Do you let him?

▲▲ As a corner is taken a striker and a defender are grappling with each other – but both are inside the goal, over the goalline. As the ball is centred, you see the striker pull the defender to the ground – just as the ball flies into the net. What now?

1

▲▲ Before a penalty is taken, you allow the defending team to swap their keeper with an outfield player who excels at saving penalties in training. Sure enough, the new keeper tips the shot round the post for a corner, which the attacking team want to take quickly. Do you delay play for the keepers to be swapped back, or allow the quick kick?

2

▲▲ A defender and a striker, both on yellow cards, chase a pass into the area. The defender lunges recklessly at the striker and misses – but the striker, seeing that the keeper will reach the ball first, reacts by diving theatrically and screaming for a red card. What action do you take, and how is play restarted?

3

▲▲ A winger rounds the keeper and centres the ball for a striker to nod it into the empty net. But before the teammate can reach it a defender steams into the back of him, knocking him out. In the process, the defender accidentally heads the ball into his own net. What now?

ANSWERS

1) The ball is out of play, so there is no reason not to allow the players to swap back. Any time lost making changes like this can simply be made up at the end of that period of play.

2) Assess this quickly and calmly. First, the defender is guilty of a reckless challenge – regardless of whether or not he made contact – so show him a second yellow card, then a red. Second, the striker is guilty of a shameful piece of simulation, so he too earns a second yellow (for unsporting behaviour) followed by a red. In terms of the restart, rewind to the first offence, which was the reckless challenge inside the area, so award a penalty-kick. There is a strong message in all this: if the striker had not tried to con you by diving, he would still be on the field, the penalty would still have been awarded, and the defender would still have been sent off. All he has gained by diving is an early bath.

3) First, call on medical aid for the striker. Second, award the goal. Third, deal with the defender. He has not denied an obvious goalscoring opportunity because the ball has gone into the net – but clearly his challenge used excessive force. Because of that, show him a red card for serious foul play.

ANSWERS

1) Nothing – unless the subs are deliberately causing a distraction by making gestures, in which case you should show them yellow cards. The location of the warm-up area is decided pre-match: you would have confirmed with both teams – based on competition rules – where the subs can exercise. This can either be behind the goal if there's space, or behind one of your two assistants. Only if the players were warming up in a non-designated area would you need to move them.

2) Award the goal. A penalty-taker is allowed to confuse opponents during free-kicks or penalty-kicks by feinting in the run-up. It's not a yellow-card offence unless you deem it unsporting behaviour – and in this scenario, that does not apply. If he had committed an unsporting act, you would show a second yellow, then a red, and, because the ball went into the net, the penalty would be retaken by a sixth player.

3) At best, this is a reckless challenge – whether or not his trailing foot was touching the ground. The fact that no contact was made is irrelevant. If you judge that he denied an obvious goalscoring opportunity, show a red card. If not, show a yellow card.

▲▲ Two of the away team's subs are warming up behind their goal, in front of their own fans. The home manager protests, saying it is distracting his strikers. What do you do?

▲▲ A player, already on a yellow card, takes his side's crucial fifth kick in a penalty shoot-out. As he runs in he stutters, does the Ali Shuffle, then blasts the ball into the net. What do you do?

▲▲ As a striker bursts clear, a defender flies in from the side with a totally committed challenge – the toe of his trailing foot touching the ground. The striker leaps into the air to avoid contact, and the defender wins possession. Play on?

1

▲▲ A goalkeeper slips as he takes a free-kick from just inside his penalty area. He miskicks the ball, which dribbles just outside the area. Seeing an opponent bearing down on him, the keeper panics, kicks the ball back into the penalty area and picks it up. The forward screams for a back-pass. What do you do?

2

▲▲ As the game goes on, you're surprised to see a player taking off his shirt to remove his thermal vest. While he's still topless the ball reaches him. He has already been booked. Do you intervene?

3

▲▲ At half-time, walking past the changing rooms, you overhear the away manager ordering his players to injure the home side's star winger and 'make sure he doesn't finish the match'. What do you do?

ANSWERS

1) It's not a back-pass, but the attacker is right to expect you to intervene: the ball has passed outside the penalty area and is therefore in play. The keeper cannot pick the ball up a second time without another player touching it first, so award an indirect free-kick, taken from where he picked it up.

2) The player shouldn't be adjusting his kit mid-match, but it's not a bookable offence: players are only cautioned for removing shirts during a goal celebration. So allow play to continue, but have a quiet word with the player to suggest that, in future, he asks permission to leave the pitch if he wants to strip off.

3) Preventative refereeing is important: do not ignore what you've heard. Before the team return to the field, make it clear that you have overheard the instructions they were given, and that you will be vigilant and take the appropriate action when needed. Make it clear to the manager that he will be reported after the game.

World Cup winners	3	(1954, 1974, 1990)
World Cup runners-up	4	(1966, 1982, 1986, 2002)
Third place	4	(1934, 1970, 2006, 2010)
Fourth place	1	(1958)
World Cup hosts	2	(1974, 2006)

* includes results representing West Germany between 1954 and 1990

Franz Beckenbauer

Beckenbauer is the only man to win the World Cup both as a player and as a manager, captaining West Germany to glory in 1974 and repeating the success as manager at Italia '90.

1970

KURT CARDS KAKHI

During an otherwise uneventful goalless draw between Mexico and Russia, the opening game of the tournament at the Aztec Stadium, in Mexico City, referee Kurt Tschenscher showed the first yellow card in World Cup history. Russian player Kakhi Asatiani had the dubious honour of being carded.

1974

CARLOS SEES RED

The players had been so well behaved at the World Cup in 1970 that the referees kept their new red card in their pockets. It didn't take long for that duck to be broken at the 1974 tournament, though. In the second half of the opening game between hosts West Germany and Chile, the Turkish referee Doğan Babacan reached for his top pocket to show Chilean striker Carlos Caszely red.

MARQUES MISTAKE

In the second round of group matches, a Brazilian referee, Armando Marques, made a blunder in officiating West Germany's 2-0 win over Yugoslavia. Marques awarded a free-kick but before the kick was taken, an opposing player committed an infringement. The referee penalised this offence and awarded a free-kick the other way. He had wrongly applied the Laws: a free-kick cannot be awarded against a team if the ball is out of play.

> West Germany emerged triumphant in the 1974 World Cup, but they lost 1-0 to neighbours East Germany in the first group stage.

> **KEITH SAYS:** 'I had the honour of presenting Jack's wife Susan with the posthumous award when Jack Taylor MBE was inducted into the National Football Museum Hall of Fame.'

Gerd Muller
Scored the winning goal in the 2–1 victory over the Netherlands in the 1974 World Cup final.

JACK AND THE MISSING FLAGS

Jack Taylor was appointed to referee the World Cup final between West Germany and the Netherlands. Jack had to be on the ball before the game had even started, spotting that the corner flags were missing. Then, after just one minute of play, he created World Cup history when he awarded a penalty-kick, the first-ever awarded in a World Cup final.

Germany's Uli Hoeness threw himself into a challenge on the right-edge of the German penalty area, felling Johan Cruyff. The spot-kick was successfully converted by Johan Neeskens.

In the 26th minute, Taylor awarded a second penalty, this time to West Germany, penalising Dutch midfielder Wim Jansen for tripping German left-midfielder Bernd Hölzenbein.

Taylor says of the incidents: 'The first penalty wasn't difficult to call. All I remember is thinking it was a 100 per cent correct decision. As Neeskens put the ball on the spot, the whole stadium went quiet. Beckenbauer, the German skipper, came to me and said, "Taylor, you're an Englishman." The kick went in and there was complete euphoria.

'What really does annoy me is the suggestion that I gave [the second penalty] to even things up. It was a trip or an attempted trip and the laws of the game are that's a penalty.'

1) There is no question of taking play back to the original foul: you rightly played the advantage, a goal was not scored and so you should restart with a corner-kick. Also, caution the defender if you deemed his challenge reckless, or send him off if you decided he used excessive force.

2) I can see the manager's point, but the Laws require a whistle to be used, so you have to reject his offer. My advice is that all referees should carry two whistles with different tones to avoid this sort of problem. I faced this situation several times in my refereeing career, so I always carried two whistles – an Acme Thunderer, which had a deep throaty sound, and my favourite Italian Balilla, which was high pitched.

3) Show him a yellow card and ask him to leave the field of play to dispose of the cigarettes and the lighter – they are not part of his approved equipment. He can only come back on during a stoppage in the game after you have checked him over.

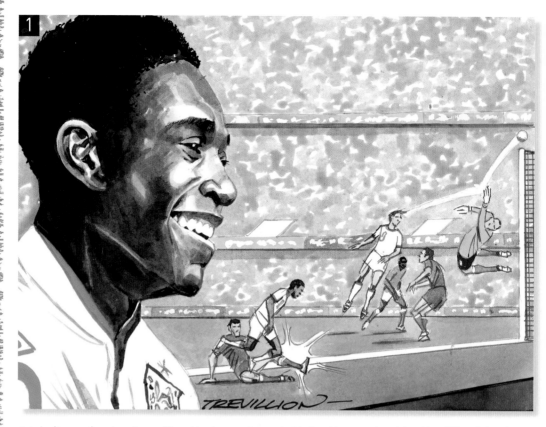

▲▲ A winger racing along the goalline whips in a great cross just before his momentum takes him off the pitch – at which point a defender deliberately clatters him from behind. But with the cross heading towards a striker you play advantage – only to see the keeper making a great save. What now?

▲▲ In a parks match the players keep being distracted by the whistle of a referee on an adjacent pitch. So the home manager hands you an old bicycle horn and asks you to use that instead. Do you agree?

▲▲ A player under tabloid scrutiny over his lifestyle celebrates a goal by producing a cigarette and ostentatiously lighting up. As you approach, he fishes out another cigarette and offers it to you. What action do you take?

1

2

3

▲▲ During a shoot-out, one of the five nominated penalty-takers, who is already on a yellow card, stutters and checks his run before firing his shot into the net. The keeper runs up to you, protesting furiously. What action do you take?

▲▲ A keeper tries to skip round an opponent, who is deliberately getting in his way, to launch a quick throw upfield. But he slips, loses the ball and the opponent slots it into the net. What now?

▲▲ A striker is jogging back from an offside position when the ball deflects out for a throw to his team. His colleague spots him and takes the throw quickly; the striker, still obviously in an offside position, controls it, turns and thrashes the ball into the net. What is your decision?

ANSWERS

1) Calm the keeper down, and make it clear that the goal is valid. The Laws state: 'Feinting to kick the ball once the player has completed his run-up is considered an act of unsporting behaviour', which would be a yellow-card offence. But stuttering or feinting during the run-up to confuse the keeper is permitted – so the penalty-taker has done nothing wrong. The keeper should read his Laws of the Game.

2) It's an indirect free-kick. The Laws make clear that 'it is an offence for a player to prevent a goalkeeper from releasing the ball from his hands' – and that clearly covers this situation, where the opponent has impeded the keeper's attempt to throw the ball to a teammate.

3) Award the goal. Although the attacker was in an offside position during the previous phase of play, and would have been penalised had he become active, the ball going out for a throw represents a new phase of play. And as you cannot be offside from a throw-in, there is no offence here to penalise.

ANSWERS

1) Disallow the goal – the spare ball is an outside agent which has clearly interfered with play. Summon the stadium manager to have the ballboy relieved of his duties, and restart play with a dropped ball at an appropriate point on the six-yard line parallel to the goalline. Include the incident in your report after the game.

2) The fact that both players squared up and brought their heads together in a confrontational way is unacceptable, as is what happened next. Show the kisser a red card for a gesture that could be deemed 'offensive, insulting and/ or abusive', and the pusher a red card for 'using excessive force' – (violent conduct).

3) You have not signalled advantage, so penalise the first offence, the foul by the defender. But this is not a red-card situation: it was not an obvious goalscoring opportunity because the forward needed to control the ball with his hand. So restart with a direct free-kick to the attacking team just outside the penalty area. Caution the defender if you deemed the challenge reckless.

▲▲ During a frantic goalmouth scramble a ballboy fires a spare ball into the melee. In a flash, one ball ends up in the net and the other flies wide. You've no idea which is which. What now?

▲▲ As two players square up after a foul, the guilty party tries to wind his rival up even more by kissing him full on the lips. The rival responds by pushing him hard in the chest twice, using both hands. What do you do?

▲▲ A striker races on to a high looped pass, beating a failed offside trap. As he runs, a defender deliberately tries to trip him, but the striker admirably stays on his feet. You prepare to signal advantage – but then spot the striker intentionally using his hand to control the ball. What now?

▼▼ A striker, already on a yellow, scores, races to the fans, and whips off his snood in celebration, waving it round his head. He's left his shirt intact. Do you intervene?

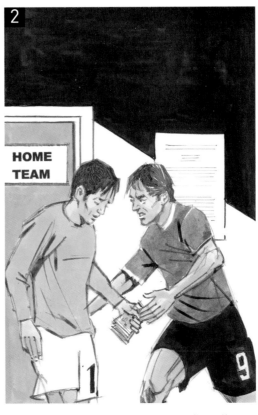

▲▲ Fifteen minutes before the game you witness the away team's star striker handing a wedge of cash to the home goalkeeper in the tunnel. You challenge them, and they claim it's purely innocent. What do you do now?

▲▲ A defender overhits a back-pass, forcing his goalkeeper to react: he tips the ball over the bar with his hand, denying a certain own goal. What now?

ANSWERS

1) Providing the player hadn't delayed the restart, and you didn't feel the celebration was excessive or provocative, then, until relatively recently, no offence would have been committed. But since the 2010 ban on snoods, he shouldn't have been wearing it in the first place.

2) You have a responsibility to uphold the integrity of the game, but you're not in a position to pass a full judgment on the players now. So make it clear to both of them that you will be reporting what you saw to the authorities after the match, and call officials from both teams to your dressing room to tell them the same.

3) Award an indirect free-kick on the goal area line parallel to the goalline, at a point nearest the position of the offence. The keeper has deliberately handled the ball from a direct kick from a teammate. He's not guilty, though, of the red-card offence of denying a goal, because keepers are allowed to handle the ball inside their own penalty area: his offence is specific.

ANSWERS

1) Was it deliberate handball? Here's the guidance you need to consider: when a ball goes to the side or above a player, and his hand or arm deliberately moves towards the ball, or he makes his body area bigger, then you should penalise for deliberate handball. But in this instance, the player's arm was already in that position, so there's no offence. Play on.

2) There's a limit on what action you can take based on allegations made during a game. All you can do for now is assure the captain who made the claim that you will report his concerns to the appropriate authorities at the end of the match. It is up to the authorities to sort this one out.

3) This is always a controversial subject, but not all swearing is the same. If you consider his comment to be offensive, insulting or abusive, show him a straight red card and stop the substitution taking place – unless they take off another player. But if you decide the comment only represents dissent, show him a yellow card, and allow the substitution to be completed. Many people advocate a zero tolerance policy on swearing – but I'm afraid that's no longer realistic.

▲▲ With five minutes left in a relegation six-pointer, the away side's captain is playing through the pain of a shoulder injury – holding his arm out away from his body as he runs. So what do you do when a goal-bound shot from the home side hits that arm and is then cleared upfield?

▲▲ During a game you notice that the away side are conceding a lot of 'soft' corners. At half-time, the opposition captain approaches you quietly and tells you he has overheard that his opponents have been bribed to concede corners as part of a spread-betting scam. What action do you take?

▲▲ A player, frustrated by a string of missed chances and some controversial decisions, is substituted late in the game. As he walks off the pitch, he swears at you. What now?

1

▼▼ In a tense penalty shoot-out the away team score with their decisive fifth kick. But, as the players race away to celebrate, you notice the kick-taker was not wearing his shinpads when he scored. What now?

2

TREVILLION

▲▲ Before a play-off final you notice the home team have included a suspended player in their starting line-up. You approach his manager, who tells you the player's red card the previous week was a joke, so he is ignoring the suspension and playing him anyway – whether you like it or not. What do you do?

3

▲▲ During a goalmouth scramble your assistant signals that the ball went over the line. You award the goal – but then spot the fourth official waving you over. He tells you he saw a TV replay in the dugout which clearly shows the ball did not go in. What now?

ANSWERS

1) You cannot stop the suspended player taking part if his club really insist on it – but they would be fools to go ahead. If the manager stands his ground, ask to see the club's chief executive, or another top-level official, and make it clear that you are aware the player is suspended, that it will be reported, and that the club is likely to face significant sanctions as a result.

2) You're not going to be popular here, but you have to apply the Laws fairly throughout. Disallow the goal, call the players back, order the kick-taker to put his shinpads on, and then allow a retake.

3) Luckily now we have goalline technology (since the 2013-14 season), this problem does not arise any more in the Premier League. But in this instance, your fourth official has put you in an impossible position. Cameras, TVs and media equipment are not allowed in the technical areas, and you need to be firm on that. As hard as it may be, accept your assistant's signal that the ball crossed the line, award the goal, then suspend the game until the TV equipment is removed. I have long been a big supporter of goalline technology.

1) Inform the chairman that, if he continues to obstruct the player, you will call the game off. If there really is a lifetime ban on the player then the police can investigate the situation after the match, as can the football authorities, based on what you include in your report – but you cannot deal with the allegation yourself. So either the player plays, or the match does not go ahead. That should focus the chairman's mind.

2) You cannot tolerate this behaviour: it's totally unacceptable. Show the player a red card for what clearly constitutes an 'offensive gesture' in the Laws. And, once the match is over, you may also want to consider reporting him to the police for indecent exposure.

3) You did not stop the game before the ball went into the net, so award the goal and immediately call medics on to attend to the keeper. There is no offence here, so no reason to penalise the attacking side – effectively this is a defensive error. Players should not be chewing gum while playing: it's obviously dangerous, and there are guidelines against it.

▲▲ Just before kick-off you discover the home team's chairman trying to eject the away side's star striker from the ground. The chairman tells you the striker was given a lifetime stadium ban a few years earlier when he was a teenage fan. What happens now?

▲▲ During half-time in a parks match you're shocked to see one of the players urinating on the pitch. What action do you take?

▲▲ As a corner is taken, the goalkeeper suddenly inhales and starts choking on his chewing gum. As he chokes, the ball flies into the net. Goal or no goal?

▲▲ To match their new tactics, the home side have widened their pitch to the maximum width. But early on a clearance hits the underside of the main stand's roof, which you realise is overhanging the touchline. The ball bounces down to a striker, who scores. What now?

▶▶ Defenders form a wall to face an indirect free-kick – then protest loudly as the attacking side form their own wall, right in front, to stop them racing out to block the shot. Do you intervene?

▲▲ A winger stumbles over the touchline as he tries to beat a defender and loses possession. The ball is cleared – but the attacking side quickly retrieve it and play it forward again towards the winger, who is still off the pitch in what would be an offside position. As he steps back onto the pitch to receive the pass, the defender has retreated, placing him onside. The winger beats the defender and scores. Is it a goal?

ANSWERS

1) There's nothing you can do about the pitch dimensions, as the match is under way. So treat this as you would if the ball struck any other outside agent: stop play and restart with a dropped ball directly beneath where it hit the roof.

2) No. This is perfectly legal. Players can stand anywhere on the field of play: the only criterion is that the defending players must be at least 9.15 metres from the ball. But clearly you need to keep an eye on what happens next – it is a potential flashpoint.

3) No. The winger did nothing wrong by leaving the pitch without permission because it was a normal part of a move. But when the ball is then played back towards him by a teammate while he remains off the field, you must treat his position as though he was standing on the touchline itself. He was effectively in an offside position, and became actively involved when he received and played the ball. The defender's movement is irrelevant. Disallow the goal, and restart with a free-kick.

ANSWERS

1) Not clever. Send all five of them off, and abandon the match as the team now have fewer than seven players. Then submit a detailed report, including your view that it looked pre-planned: the authorities have the option of recording the final score as 4-0. There is no rule that if a team causes an abandonment then they forfeit the game. So the result is likely to be relegation, fines and suspensions all round.

2) Provided the comment has not been overheard by others who may be offended, manage the situation with a strong rebuke. Let them know that if you hear a repeat, they will be reported to the authorities. But if the comment was loud enough to be heard by others, send off the player who made it. It would then be up to him to appeal, with his team-mate supporting him at the hearing.

3) Send off the defender for denying an obvious goalscoring opportunity. Restart with a direct free-kick if the attacker was hit outside the area, or a penalty if he was inside.

▲▲ The away side, who need to lose by three goals or fewer to stay up, go 4-0 down late on. Immediately five of their players run over to you and take turns to shout foul abuse. It looks pre-planned: they want five red cards, an abandonment, and the result recorded as a 3-0 defeat. What now?

▼▼ A player refers to a teammate by a term you consider to be racially charged. Realising you have overheard, both players immediately try to assure you that it was an in-joke between friends, and no offence was intended or taken. Do you take any action?

▲▲ A defender, off the field for treatment, sees an opposition striker burst through on goal. So he grabs a spare ball from a ballboy and boots it straight at the striker, knocking him over. A clear goalscoring chance is gone. What now?

1

▲▲ The away team arrive at the ground without their kit – so the home chairman offers them his team's second strip. Both managers are happy, but the kit has the home players' names and sponsor's logo. What now?

2

▲▲ You play advantage after a foul by the home team. But as the away team race upfield, one of their players fouls an opponent – and the ball breaks back to the home team. Can you play a second advantage?

3

▲▲ The attacking side play a ball through to their striker, who is clearly in an offside position. But before it reaches him a defender tries to intercept, and deflects the ball past his keeper into the net. How does play restart?

ANSWERS

1) Your priority has to be to get the game played, for the fans, media and teams. The kit is a different colour, so there are no safety issues – but you do need to deal with the names, to reduce confusion, and the sponsor's logo, to avoid contractual problems. Your easiest solution is to have the players turn the tops inside out.

2) The fact that the away team have made progress upfield means the advantage has been taken, so the game continues, unless it was a red-card offence. Treat the second incident in the normal way. You must be careful, though: playing successive advantages means you run the risk of losing control.

3) With a kick-off to the defending side: it's an own goal. The striker has not touched the ball, so is not interfering with play. Only if you felt he had clearly distracted or deceived the defender would you penalise him for being in an offside position – but that distraction needs to be very obvious for you to take action. You are not a mind reader.

ARGENTINA

World Cup winners	2	(1978, 1986)
World Cup runners-up	2	(1930, 1990)
Third place	-	
Fourth place	-	
World Cup hosts	1	(1978)

Diego Maradona

Maradona won the World Cup for Argentina virtually single-handedly in 1986 (with a little help from the 'Hand of God'), and his 66-yard dribble to score his wonder goal against England was later voted Goal of the Century by Fifa.com voters. He was less successful as Argentina's manager, selecting a mind-boggling total of 108 players over 18 months in qualification for the 2010 World Cup finals. His bizarre management seemed more a hindrance than a help to Lionel Messi and co. who were eventually beaten 4-0 by Germany in the quarter-finals.

1978

TRIGGER LIPS THOMAS

Brazil drew their first-round match with Sweden at the World Cup finals in Argentina. But Welsh referee Clive Thomas upset the entire Brazilian nation when he blew for full-time an instant before Zico headed the ball into the net, and didn't allow what would have been the winning goal to stand. The fact that the linesman had made Nelinho reposition the ball before swinging in the corner-kick for Zico to score, wasting valuable seconds, made it all the worse. Thomas's decision did not prove crucial in the end, though, as Brazil went on to qualify for the second phase.

STICKY (PLASTER) SITUATION

The final at the Monumental Stadium, Buenos Aires, was delayed when Argentinean players protested about the plaster cast that Dutchman René van der Kerkhof was wearing to protect two broken bones. Italian referee Sergio Gonella (later taken off FIFA's list of approved referees) asked for it to be removed, unnecessarily causing the match to kick off seven minutes late, but then allowed him to play with an extra layer of bandages wrapped around it.

Osvaldo Ardiles

'Ossie' Ardiles won 63 caps for the national team, including playing in Argentina's victorious World Cup winning squad of 1978.

ANSWERS

1) It is not handball as the ball was not in play – but you still need to intervene. When you award an attacking free-kick near the penalty area, you go through a clear process: positioning the ball, telling the attacking players to leave it where it is and that they may only take the kick on your signal, then positioning the wall. This player has ignored you, so show him a yellow card for unsporting behaviour, then restart with the original free-kick.

2) Show the defender a yellow card for delaying the restart. And show the kick-taker a red card for violent conduct – this is clearly a deliberately violent act. Restart with a direct free-kick to the defence.

3) Regardless of the keeper's juggling, this is still a deliberate back-pass which has been deliberately handled. Award an indirect free-kick to the attacking side, taken from the point where the keeper picked up the ball – or, if that point was inside the six-yard box, from the nearest point on the six-yard line parallel to the goalline.

TREVILLION

▲▲ A player is about to take a direct free-kick. He has placed the ball and you have blown the whistle – but the player then picks the ball up again to reposition it. The wall shouts for handball. What do you do?

▲▲ A player who has committed a foul on the edge of his penalty area hears you give permission for a quick free-kick – so stands right in front of the ball. The taker reacts by blasting the ball at his groin. What do you do?

▶▶ A defender turns to pass the ball back to his keeper but miskicks it: the ball looks like it is looping up over the keeper's head. So the keeper jumps, heads the ball, deflects it onto his crossbar then picks up the rebound. What is the correct decision?

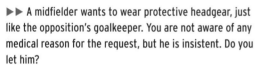

▲▲ Early in a Conference game you are stunned to see a physio punch an opposing sub. When you order him out of the technical area he points out that he's the only trained medic on either bench. What now?

▶▶ A midfielder wants to wear protective headgear, just like the opposition's goalkeeper. You are not aware of any medical reason for the request, but he is insistent. Do you let him?

TREVILLION

▲▲ With his side 5-0 up, a maverick striker strolls up to take a penalty, then stops in front of the ball. In one movement, he scoops the ball up on to his instep and managers to flick it past the baffled goalkeeper. Opponents are outraged. Is it a goal?

ANSWERS

1) Continue without him. It's not ideal, but many matches are played without physios – and even at professional level, unless competition rules state otherwise, it is your call whether to play on without medical staff. I would never abandon a game if it can be avoided. So send the physio out of the technical area, tell him he may still be needed in an emergency, and complete the match as normal. Afterwards, make sure you have full notes of what happened, as this could become a police matter.

2) If a player asks to wear anything more than the basic equipment it needs to be obviously necessary (such as a cast to protect an injured wrist), and it must not pose a danger to opposing players or himself. So in this case, having spoken to his manager to confirm there is no valid medical reason for the headgear, refuse permission.

3) If he genuinely manages to pull this trick off – the ball staying in contact with his instep throughout one, single movement, it is a valid goal – players can lift the ball with one or both feet when taking a free-kick. But you must be sure he has not played the ball twice. If he has, it's an indirect free-kick to the defending team.

ANSWERS

1) Law 3 deals with this sort of situation specifically, making it clear that if a change of goalkeepers is made without your permission, you must caution both the individuals involved. You also need to ask the new goalkeeper to leave the field of play so that the substitution can be completed properly. Then, restart with a corner-kick. An alternative valid interpretation is that the sub keeper came on to the field of play without your permission, whereas the original keeper had left the field of play at half-time with your permission. If you prefer that line of reasoning, the keeper is not cautioned but the sub keeper is.

2) Your assistant is guilty of improper conduct - it's totally unacceptable behaviour: officials have to be impartial and totally transparent. Replace him with the fourth official, find a qualified replacement fourth official if possible, and report the full facts to the appropriate authorities.

3) It's a goal. Why penalise the attacking side by disallowing it? Show the defender a yellow card, not a red: he is guilty of unsporting behaviour, but clearly not guilty of preventing a goal.

1

▲▲ In the first minute of the second half, the away keeper makes a stunning save, tipping the ball over the bar. But only then do you realise that he's not the same keeper who played in the first half. What now?

2

▲▲ Before kick-off you spot your assistant telling one of the players what a huge fan he is and asking for an autograph. The opposition manager notices too and is furious. What do you do?

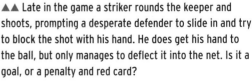

3

▲▲ Late in the game a striker rounds the keeper and shoots, prompting a desperate defender to slide in and try to block the shot with his hand. He does get his hand to the ball, but only manages to deflect it into the net. Is it a goal, or a penalty and red card?

▲▲ In the last minute of a bitter derby the home captain launches into a violent two-footed lunge right by the touchline – just feet away from where police are struggling to keep rival fans apart. A red card now could spark mayhem in the stands. What do you do?

▲▲ The ball goes out for a corner, so you signal for a player who has been receiving treatment behind the net to come back on. But he delays his re-entry briefly until the corner is taken, then dashes on, unmarked, and heads the ball into the net. What now?

▲▲ A striker staggers his penalty run-up to try to fool the goalkeeper into diving early – but the keeper doesn't even flinch. So the taker has a rethink, stops, and walks back to start his run again. Do you let him?

ANSWERS

1) You cannot let an intimidating atmosphere put you off applying the Laws in a consistent and fair way. Show the courage of your convictions, trust the police and stewards, and send the captain off. If it provokes serious trouble in the crowd you have the option of abandoning the game. Either way, report everything that happened to the authorities.

2) He's trying to be clever, but he hasn't read the Laws. He is allowed to return to the field of play on your signal from any position – including from behind the goalline – when the ball is out of play. But when it's in play, he can only return from the touchline. So disallow the goal, caution the player for re-entering the field of play without permission, and restart with an indirect free-kick from where the ball was when play was stopped.

3) No. It's clearly unsporting behaviour: show him a yellow card, making it very clear that a penalty run-up needs to be one uninterrupted movement. Restart with the original penalty-kick.

73

1) The fact that this is a clear scoring opportunity does make a difference. If the ball was in a neutral area of the pitch you would stop play immediately, prioritising player safety, and would restart with a dropped ball. But the Laws do allow you to play on 'if the outside agent does not interfere with play' – so in these circumstances, it makes sense to wait for things to resolve themselves. If he scores, restart with a kick-off. If not, stop the game.

2) Playing on with a corner of the pitch in darkness is not an option – there are broadcasters and a paying crowd who are entitled to be able to see the game. Take the players off and talk to the stadium manager. I was at a live TV game between Braga and Benfica when the floodlights failed three times in the first half. The referee dealt with it brilliantly and patiently – eventually bringing the game to a conclusion after 20 minutes of stoppage time.

3) I would smile and escort him off the pitch – there's no need to cause a scene. But, as always, you need to apply the Laws: he had no right to enter the field of play and his action with the glasses was insulting – so report him to the authorities.

1

▲▲ As the away team close in on a goal, a home fan vaults the hoardings and races into the penalty area. Your assistant flags to make sure you've see him. If you stop play, you will be preventing a clear goalscoring opportunity. What do you do?

2

▲▲ In the 80th minute of a game, one of the floodlights fails. You stop play, but both managers want to finish the match. One corner of the pitch is very dark. Should you continue?

3

▲▲ At the end of the game a disgruntled manager walks on to the pitch and, in front of the TV cameras, offers you a pair of glasses, saying: 'Happy new year!' What do you do?

▲▲ A player recently caught up in a racism controversy scores a goal and pulls his shirt off in celebration. On his chest is an anti-racism slogan. What do you do?

▲▲ A defender chases a ball towards his own corner. Unsure who got the last touch on it, he shouts to your assistant for advice and is told it will be a goal-kick if the ball goes out – so he shepherds it out of play. Opponents are angry, claiming the assistant gave him an unfair advantage. What now?

▲▲ A defender sends a back-pass short and a striker races on to it. The keeper dives and gets both hands on the ball. The striker wants the keeper sent off for denying an obvious goalscoring opportunity – but the keeper says it's just an indirect free-kick. What do you award?

ANSWERS

1) Show him a yellow card. The Laws are clear: 'A player must be cautioned if he removes his shirt or covers his head with his shirt' and players must not display 'slogans or advertising'. There are very rare occasions when you could use common sense on this – such as in November 2011, when referee Darren Deadman rightly allowed Billy Sharp to display a T-shirt tribute following the death of his son – but as a rule it cannot be left to individual officials to make value judgments on political or personal slogans. Caution him, and report the facts to the authorities after the game.

2) Opponents are understandably upset – but what happened does not alter how play should restart: it is still a legitimate goal-kick. You need to have a quick word with your assistant about his error of judgment, and tell the complainers to get on with the game.

3) It's an indirect free-kick for the handling of a deliberate back-pass. It's not a red-card offence because a keeper is allowed to handle the ball in his own area: his only offence is handling the back-pass.

1) It's a goal. The same law applies in a shoot-out as for a penalty in extended time: 'A goal is awarded if, before passing between the goalposts and under the crossbar, the ball touches either or both of the goalposts and/or the crossbar and/or the goalkeeper.' You decide when the kick has been completed, but you must allow the ball to finish its course. If it's any consolation to the keeper, he can expect many millions of hits on YouTube . . .

2) Award the free-kick – but not because the keeper handled the ball. Once the ball hits the ground it is in play, so it's fine for the keeper to gain possession with his hands. However, that only applies when the dropped ball is uncontested, as they often are inside the area. In this situation, the keeper is guilty of dangerous play because his action caused danger to himself, so award an indirect free-kick against the defending side.

3) Award the goal. You'd have to be very certain that a deliberate unsporting act had been committed to disallow it. Calm the players down, make the keeper aware that you understand what has been alleged, and include it all in your report.

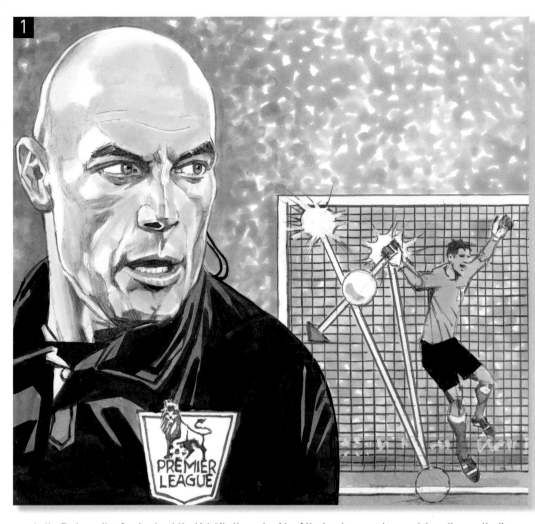

1

▲▲ In the final penalty of a shoot-out the kick hits the underside of the bar, bounces down and doesn't cross the line. The keeper raises his arms to celebrate – and ends up punching the ball into his net. What is your decision?

2

▲▲ A striker and a keeper contest a dropped ball inside the area. As soon as the ball hits the ground, the keeper smothers it – his head ending up inches from the striker's boot. The attacking team are angry and want an indirect free-kick. What now?

3

▲▲ As a keeper tries to catch a looping corner, a striker next to him lets out a massive sneeze. The surprised keeper fumbles the ball, allowing another striker to score. There's an uproar, and you spot the attackers laughing. What do you do?

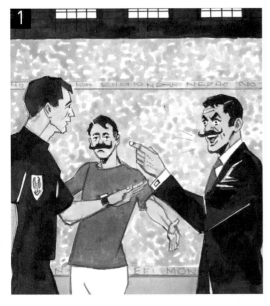

▲▲ A striker who has fallen out with his manager runs out for a televised game wearing a comedy moustache, mocking his boss's facial hair. The manager demands you delay the game until the player removes it. What now?

▶▶ A feud between two players escalates with the defender shoving his hand into the striker's face. As he does so, the striker bites two of the defender's fingers. What action do you take?

▲▲ Two players challenge for the ball, which then rolls towards the keeper. As he goes to collect it, the keeper screams to your assistant to ask if he can pick it up. The assistant shouts 'yes' – but when the keeper grabs the ball you blow for a free-kick. There's an outcry. What now?

ANSWERS

1) This really isn't your problem. While the comedy moustache does count as an addition to his equipment, it doesn't constitute a clear danger to the player or opponents, so there are no grounds to intervene or delay the game. If he thinks this is the best way of improving his relationship with his boss, let him carry on. It is up to the club to resolve it.

2) I'm sure the striker will argue he would not have bitten the fingers had he not been shoved in the face – but that does not change what he did: clearly both players are guilty of violent conduct, so show them both red cards. And, as the defender committed the first offence, restart with a free-kick to the attacking team.

3) It's your call. If you know for certain that this was a back-pass then you have to go ahead and award an indirect free-kick from where the ball was picked up. But you also need to have a serious word with your assistant – officials should never instruct players what to do – and apologise to the goalkeeper too, though he should also know not to ask officials for advice.

1) A great question. Allow the substitution to go ahead. The key factor here is that he did not use offensive, insulting or abusive language towards you. Although managers are not shown cards, that would have been the equivalent of a red-card offence – meaning he could take no further part in any capacity. But his offence here was dissent, so, when you sent him to the stand, you would have made clear that, should he wish to come on as a player later in the game, he would do so with a yellow card to his name. Make a full report of what happened after the game.

2) Order a retake. To disallow the goal you must be convinced that the flicking lights were an outside interference which had a direct influence on the passage of play. In this case, both the penalty-taker and goalkeeper were clearly distracted, so a retake is fair.

3) As tempting as it may be to take advantage of the goalkeeper's sporting advice, the Laws make clear that if both officials have not seen the whole of the ball cross the line, a goal cannot be given. But have a word with the keeper, and thank him for his good intentions.

▲▲ A player-manager in the technical area keeps having a go at you. He doesn't swear but carries on ranting, so you send him to the stand. Minutes later you see him back on the touchline in playing kit, trying to come on as a sub. What now?

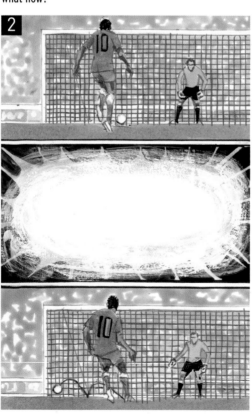

▲▲ It's a penalty. As the taker races in to strike the ball, a floodlight behind the goal flickers off and on. He scuffs his shot and keeper makes no effort to save it – both assume you'll award a retake. But the goal goes in. What now?

▲▲ In a late goalmouth scramble, the ball crosses the goalline before being booted clear. Attackers scream for a goal, but your view was blocked and your assistant is unsure. The keeper, whose side are 4-0 up, sportingly admits it did go in. What now?

1 ▲▲ It's a late corner. To shield his eyes from the sun the keeper has put a baseball cap on – but as the ball is whipped in, an opponent knocks it off. Dazzled, the keeper misses the ball and the striker heads it into the net. There's an uproar. What now?

▼▼ A keeper scrambles to reach a ball on the edge of the area. To control it, he reaches his hand outside the penalty area and drags the ball back towards him. A sliver of the ball was overlapping the line. Do you intervene?

2

3 ▲▲ A keeper saves a penalty but one of the taker's teammates, who has encroached, slots home the rebound. Defenders are furious – but the attacker insists encroachment is only an offence if the penalty is scored directly. What now?

ANSWERS

1) Award the goal. You need to assess whether the striker deliberately knocked the cap off. In my view, he is not guilty of that: his back is to the keeper, and he makes clean contact with the ball. If you judged it was deliberate you would disallow the goal, caution the opponent for unsporting behaviour and restart with a direct free-kick, but I think this challenge looks fair.

2) The width of the line marking the area forms part of the area, so the goalkeeper has – just about – not committed an offence. If the whole of the ball was outside the line, though, you would award a direct free-kick, and, if he had denied an obvious goalscoring opportunity, a red card.

3) The attacker is right that you would have punished encroachment with a retake had the penalty been scored directly. But he's wrong to think that encroachment is fine in other circumstances. Award an indirect free-kick to the defending team, to be taken from the point where the attacker encroached. Everyone other than the keeper and the taker must be at least 9.15 metres from the ball when the kick is taken: no exceptions.

ITALY

World Cup winners	4	(1934, 1938, 1982, 2006)
World Cup runners-up	2	(1970, 1994)
Third place	1	(1990)
Fourth place	1	(1978)
World Cup hosts	2	(1934, 1990)

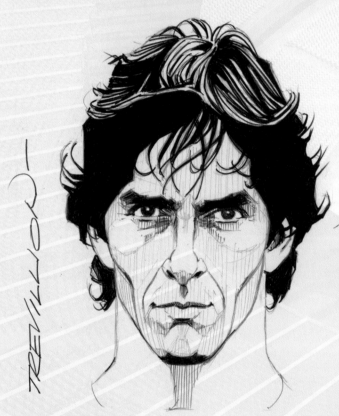

Paolo Rossi

This lethal finisher won it all in 1982, helping Italy to the World Cup title, scoring six goals to claim the Golden Boot as the tournament's top-scorer, and being named the player of the tournament. Only Mario Kempes of Argentina, in 1978, has claimed the same hat-trick.

Paolo Maldini

Maldini retired after the 2002 World Cup as Italy's most capped player with 126 international appearances, including 74 as his country's captain. While this elegant defender never lifted the World Cup, it is a measure of his stature in the game that in 2002, he was voted by fans as one of three defenders in FIFA's all-time World Cup dream team, alongside Roberto Carlos and Franz Beckenbauer.

1982

PHANTOM WHISTLER CONFUSES STUPAR

A group match between France and Kuwait at Spain '82 descended into farce in the 81st minute when Michel Platini played Alain Giresse in to score. As Platini played the through ball, a loud whistle was clearly audible, causing the Kuwaiti defenders to pause momentarily, thinking that Giresse had been ruled offside. But the whistle had not been blown by Russian ref Miroslav Stupar, and he allowed the goal.

The Kuwait captain, Saad Al-Houti, headed to the touchline, presumably to ask his manager to lodge a protest. Meanwhile, furious Kuwaiti FA president Prince Fahid left his seat in the stand above the dugouts to complain and threaten to withdraw his team. After eight minutes of mayhem, Stupar, a 40-year-old professor of physical education from Moscow, changed his initial decision, cancelling the goal, and restarted the game with a dropped ball 10 yards outside Kuwait's penalty area. He was wrong – under the existing Laws of the Game, the goal should have been awarded.

Stupar was subsequently removed by FIFA from their list of referees, and Fahid was fined $14,000 for his part in the unseemly shenanigans.

SCHUMACHER IRONS OUT BATTISTON

Another perfect through ball by French midfield maestro Michel Platini caused more controversy in France's semi-final versus West Germany. With the game poised at 1-1, French substitute Patrick Battiston, who'd only been on the field for six minutes, ran onto Platini's pass. German keeper Harald Schumacher raced out and, unable to beat Battiston to the ball, he followed through and played the man instead. Battiston was poleaxed, his shot trickled wide and he had to be stretchered

off. Incredibly, referee Charles George Rainier Corver of the Netherlands took no action at all – Schumacher wasn't even cautioned and the game restarted with a goal-kick.

The incident happened in the 56th minute when the score was 1-1, also the score at full-time. A thrilling period of extra-time ended 3-3, with West Germany edging the penalty shoot-out 5-4 to reach the final. But if Schumacher had been correctly sent off, would West Germany still have won?

Schumacher's violent assault was condemned worldwide. A German newspaper even offered Battiston a week's holiday to recuperate.

1) Depending on the severity of the hacking offence, caution or send off the defender. It is not a straight red card for denying an obvious goalscoring opportunity though, because the ball was not in play – it had not left the penalty area. So, having dealt with the defender, restart with a retaken goal-kick.

2) One of the players has committed a deliberate offence, one has not. So show the defender a red card for deliberately spitting at an opponent. The striker's act might not have been pleasant, but it was not deliberate, so there is no action to take against him. Restart play with a penalty to the attacking team.

3) You are still within your rights to change your decision because play has not restarted. So disallow the goal, and, if the crossbar cannot be repaired or replaced, abandon the game – unless there is an alternative pitch available. Report what happened to the relevant authorities – this could have been a very serious incident.

1

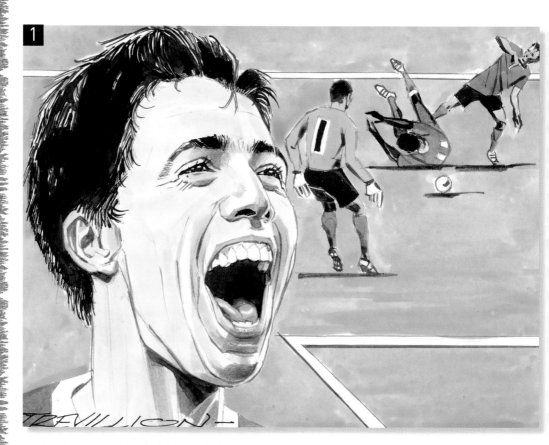

▲▲ The keeper stumbles as he takes a goal-kick. As the ball dribbles forwards, a striker races towards it – but before he reaches the ball, still inside the area, a chasing defender hacks him down. What happens now?

2

▲▲ A striker scuffs a sitter inside the six-yard box and spits in disgust. But the spit is caught by a gust of wind and hits a defender – who furiously spits back at him. You stop play and race over. What now?

3

▲▲ It's a penalty in a junior match. As the taker runs in, the keeper suddenly rushes off his line, shouting that the wooden crossbar is creaking in the wind. The shot goes in, so you give the goal – but seconds later the crossbar crashes down. What now?

▲▲ Awaiting a corner, a defender decides to stretch from the crossbar. But his arm catches in the net and you don't notice until the corner is taken. The ball, headed at goal, strikes his arm and deflects to safety. What now?

▲▲ In a non-league game you're shocked to see a long punt upfield bounce into an unguarded net. You then realise that the keeper, a qualified medic, is behind the net helping treat an elderly fan who has collapsed. What action do you take?

▲▲ During the warm-ups, as you jog around with your assistants you are shocked to see a fight between two home players. Both players, named in the starting XI, throw punches. What now?

ANSWERS

1) You should have spotted this before signalling for the kick to be taken, but it's too late now. Award a penalty and show the dangling defender a red card. Clearly it's not 'hand to ball', but his arm was raised in an unnatural position and stopped a goal being scored. The defender should be focused on the game.

2) Clearly there are two priorities: first, make sure the fan is being tended to and that other medical help is on the way, and second, apply the Laws of the Game fairly. I would not allow the goal, on the basis that the Laws state a team must have a goalkeeper. If the keeper had left the field as part of normal play (for instance if his momentum had taken him over the goalline) you would treat the situation differently, but here the keeper is missing for a reason that cannot be considered part of play. As the ball was in the net, restart with a dropped ball from where it was punted upfield.

3) Dismiss both. The fact that play has not started is irrelevant: the players are under your jurisdiction. Their manager can nominate two of his named substitutes to step up to start the game, but they cannot be replaced on the bench.

ANSWERS

1) Once you have terminated a game, you cannot reverse a previous decision, or resume play: that is clear in law. Besides which, you saw the incident, decided there was no offence and played on – and it is your judgment, ultimately, which counts.

2) Call their captain over, and make it clear that the injured player cannot return to the field until the game has restarted – so he cannot take the kick (unless there is a need for a retake). If his teammates still refuse to take it, make it clear to them that the game will be abandoned. That should focus minds.

3) This isn't something you can deal with during the match: it's the club's responsibility to ensure that their players are allowed to take part. If they want to, they can substitute the player, but if they decide to keep him on, that's their call too. You just need to make sure that both clubs know the situation, and that you will be making a full report to the authorities after the game.

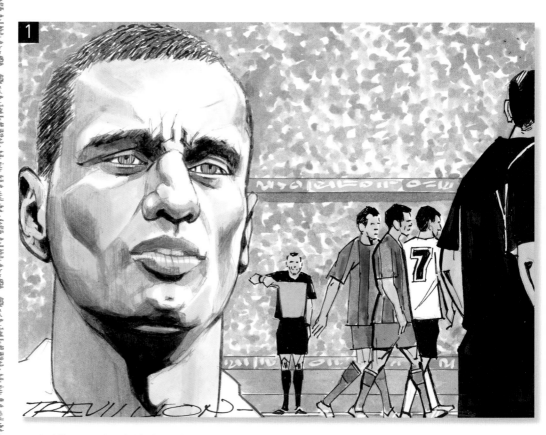

▲▲ A striker goes down in the box but you wave play on. As the ball is cleared upfield you blow for full-time - but then see your assistant signalling for a penalty. He tells you he started flagging before you blew up. What now?

▲▲ It's a penalty – but the team's penalty specialist, hurt in the incident, is off the pitch receiving treatment. The other players refuse to take the kick until he returns, saying that would unfairly penalise them. What do you do?

▲▲ At half-time, the away side's manager runs over in a panic: he says a club official has just told him that his right-back shouldn't be playing due to the number of yellow cards he has accumulated. What now?

▲▲ A player who has been out with a neck injury comes off the bench wearing what looks like a neck brace. The physio says it is safe and padded, and he is fit to take part – but opponents say it's a danger. What do you do?

▲▲ Seeing a shot fired in at goal, a defender on the goalline instinctively reaches up and catches it. Realising what he has done, he quickly drops the ball back over his head into the net, before you can blow your whistle. What now?

▲▲ A striker, already on a yellow card, tries an elaborate backheel but completely misses the ball. Instead, his foot connects with a defender behind him, who falls over with blood streaming from his knee. What action do you take?

1) There is no way he can play wearing that sort of equipment. It is not a question of whether or not he is medically fit to play – that is not your call. It's about whether the item represents a danger to himself or his opponents. This sort of collar clearly falls into the same category as snoods, which were outlawed in 2010 because of the risk of them being caught as players run. Tell the player and his manager that the collar must be removed, and remind the player that, if he continues without it, he does so at his own risk.

2) The player has saved himself from a red card, but has cost his team a goal. Had he not thrown it into the net then clearly you would have dismissed him and awarded a penalty. As it is, show him a yellow card for unsporting behaviour and award the goal.

3) Your first priority, of course, is to get the medical staff on to see to the injured player, and to make sure he stays off the pitch until the bleeding has stopped. As for the striker: his action was careless rather than reckless, and there was no malice, so there is no reason to show him a second yellow card. Restart with a direct free-kick.

1) Referees are directed to stop play for any serious injury – the safety of players always comes first. But before making any such decision you need to be 100 per cent certain that the injury is both serious and genuine: it is rarely a snap decision unless a head injury is involved. In this case, the time it takes for you to assess the injury would also be time enough for the ball to bounce into the net. Award the goal and then call the physio on.

2) Stop play. Players cannot take part in active play without boots – he is putting himself in danger, regardless of any chest-high challenges he may choose to make. Ask him to leave the field. He can only return when the ball is next out of play and you have checked his footwear. Restart with an indirect free-kick against the midfielder's side, for the offence of dangerous play.

3) Yes. It may seem harsh in the circumstances, but the keeper has taken possession of the ball after a deliberate pass to him by a teammate – and that's not allowed. It's an indirect free-kick to the attacking team.

1

TREVILLION

▲▲ A keeper, seeing a striker shaping up to lob him, races backwards, but trips and horribly twists his knee. He falls to the floor screaming. Do you stop play, or wait until the ball bounces into the net?

2

3

▲▲ A player's boot comes off but, instead of stopping, he plays on and launches a chest-high challenge for the ball. It looks wild – but he wasn't wearing studs, and won the ball cleanly. What now?

▶▶ A defender badly overhits a back-pass: the ball strikes the post and rebounds back to the keeper, who catches it instinctively then clears it upfield. Do you intervene?

▲▲ A player commits two yellow-card fouls during the same passage of play, but both times you have played advantage. What do you do when the ball next goes out?

▲▲ In wet, muddy conditions, the home keeper has been using a towel to dry his gloves. But a lobbed shot catches him out: still holding the towel, he dives and tips the ball behind to safety. What now?

▲▲ The away side are 2-0 up but have had four red cards and used all their subs. So when their captain goes down injured with five minutes left, he asks if he can stay sitting in the centre circle to avoid the game being abandoned. What do you do?

1) It's a penalty. On the line counts as part of the penalty area, so the decision is clear-cut. And, if you believe the defender has denied an obvious goalscoring opportunity, send him off.

2) Stop play. It may seem unfair, but you can't award goals out of sympathy: the only time a goal is scored is if the whole of the ball crosses the goalline between the posts and under the bar. So, calm the players down, have the goal frame repositioned, then restart with a dropped ball on the six-yard line parallel to the goalline, at a point nearest to where the player collided with the post.

3) Send off the six substitutes for violent conduct, making sure they leave the technical area, well away from the playing area. This does not change the number of players on the pitch, nor the number of substitutions both teams can make: they simply have fewer options on the bench. Restart with a dropped ball and, after the match, request that the authorities view footage of the incident to be sure that all the guilty players were dismissed. Both clubs can expect further sanctions.

1

TREVILLION.

▲▲ A striker evades a sliding tackle from the last defender – but, as he races past, the defender manages to stop the ball with his hand. The ball was on, not over, the 18-yard line. What now?

2

▲▲ In a youth match, a defender collides with the wooden goalposts as he tries a last-ditch clearance. The contact knocks the post inwards – enough to block the goal-bound shot. What do you do?

3

▲▲ During a heated game you are stunned to see a mass brawl break out by the benches. You stop play and, with your assistants, identify three subs from both sides who all threw punches. What do you do?

▲▲ It's a foul – but you've dropped your whistle and can't find your spare. As you desperately race upfield to stop play, a defender picks the whistle up and blows it. Most players stop, but a striker racing in on goal is brutally hacked down. What now?

▲▲ A striker leaps athletically towards a high cross and accidentally clatters into the back of a teammate. The action keeps him in the air just long enough to let him power a header into the net. Is it a goal?

▲▲ In wet conditions, a striker is close in on goal, one-on-one with the keeper – who deliberately flicks water at him to put him off. The water misses, but the striker still fluffs his shot. What do you do?

ANSWERS

1) What a mess. You need to deal with every element of what happened. Calm the players down, retrieve your whistle, and bring play back to the original foul, which is where you should restart the game. However, you also need to take action against the hacking defender: send him off for violent conduct. It's irrelevant that play was technically not live at the time. And finally, make sure you locate your spare whistle – and don't lose it again.

2) Yes. This was not a deliberate attempt to gain extra height, or to piggyback – which would have represented unsporting behaviour. It was a legitimate move by both players, resulting in an accidental collision.

3) It may only be water, but the keeper is technically guilty of deliberately throwing an object at the striker, which, in the Laws, constitutes attempting to strike an opponent. So, in this situation you don't need to consider whether or not the keeper's action denied an obvious goalscoring opportunity, because trying to strike an opponent, even if there is no contact, is a red-card offence on its own. So send him off and award a penalty.

89

1) The manager deserves some leeway. With the clock stopped, allow him a reasonable amount of time to retrieve his sulking player. If the player does return to the pitch he can continue to play because the substitution had not been completed. If he stays in the dressing room, the substitution can take place. Either way, his embarrassing overreaction means he receives a yellow card for leaving the field of play without permission.

2) If you are certain the ball was going in, show the defender a red card. In this situation the boot is considered an extension of the player's hand, so this is deliberate handball, denying a clear goal. Restart play with a penalty-kick.

3) You need to deal with any allegation made between teams off the field openly and swiftly. Tell the home manager about the claim, ask him to confirm that he has not made any changes, and ask both twins to confirm their names. If they all insist no swap has been made, that is as far as you can take it in the time available. Restart the game in the normal way and report what happened so that the authorities can investigate later.

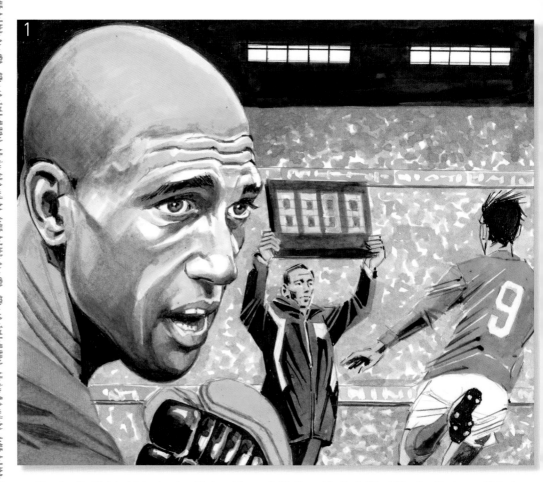

▲▲ Your fourth official mistakenly raises his board for a substitution while the ball is still in play. The home side's star striker is furious to see his number come up – and when you then award his team a penalty, he refuses to take it and storms off down the tunnel instead. His manager asks you to delay the kick while he tries to drag the player back on. What now?

▲▲ A defender's boot comes loose as he makes a last-ditch attempt to stop a ball rolling into his unguarded net. Instinctively, he picks the boot up and hurls it at the ball, deflecting it out of play to safely. What action do you take, and how does play restart?

▲▲ At half-time the away manager tells you he has information that the home club – who have a pair of identical twin defenders – have swapped them during the break without making an official substitution. The home manager denies it, and it's time to restart. What do you do?

1

▲▲ A penalty-taker trips and misses the ball completely. As the keeper howls with laughter, the striker picks himself up and starts to walk back to take it again – but as he passes the ball he suddenly backheels it into the net. Everyone looks at you. What now?

2

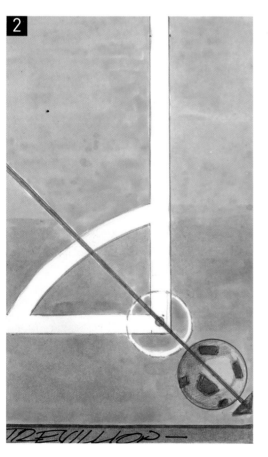

3

▲▲ A team from New Zealand start to perform an intimidating Haka dance, delaying kick-off. You haven't given permission, and the TV company wants the match started. What do you do?

◄◄ The away team try to run down the clock by keeping the ball in the opposition's corner – but a home defender manages to get a foot to it, blasting it out of play. The ball strikes the flagpost dead centre, knocking it out of the ground. The away side want a corner, the home side say it's a throw. What is your decision?

ANSWERS

1) It's a clever attempt to save face, but it's not a goal. A penalty involves one movement to kick the ball forward; he has effectively taken two run-ups to the same kick. Caution (a yellow card) the taker for unsporting behaviour, and order a retake. You should have avoided this situation by blowing your whistle the moment he fell over.

2) Technically, it's a dropped ball – that's what the law states if the referee isn't sure. But in practice most referees wouldn't want to appear so indecisive: it's sensible to make a decision one way or the other, and in this case the least controversial option is to give the throw.

3) On paper, you should intervene – but clearly this is a sensitive situation. Although they have delayed the start, out of respect to the tradition you should allow the Haka to be completed. But make it clear that you will report the matter to the competition: this should have been pre-agreed, with time allowed for the Haka so that the match was not delayed.

NETHERLANDS

World Cup winners	-	
World Cup runners-up	3	(1974, 1978, 2010)
Third place	-	
Fourth place	1	(1998)
World Cup hosts	-	

Johan Cruyff

Awarded the Golden Ball as the player of the tournament in 1974, Cruyff epitomised the Dutch 'Total Football' philosophy, which won football fans' hearts and carried them to the final. At the start of that final, the Netherlands completed 13 passes ending with a foul on Cruyff and a penalty awarded before West Germany had even touched the ball.

1986

PEN CHANGE

During the 1986 World Cup quarter-final penalty shoot-out between Brazil and France, Bruno Bellone's shot hit a goalpost, rebounded out, hit the goalkeeper and rebounded into the net. Romanian ref Ioan Igna did not count it as a miss. Brazil's captain, Edinho, was cautioned for protesting and France won the shoot-out 4-3.

A year later, the penalty law was amended as follows: 'At the taking of a penalty-kick a goal shall not be nullified if, before passing through the posts and under the crossbar, the ball touches either or both of the goalposts, or the crossbar, or the goalkeeper, or any combination of these agencies.'

THE HAND OF DIEGO

Diego Maradona scored two memorable goals in Argentina's 2-1 quarter-final win over England – the second, a spectacular dribble from inside his own half, remembered for all the right reasons, but the crucial opener, his infamous 'Hand of God' flick over Peter Shilton, will always grate with England fans.

The officials that day were referee Ali Bin Nasser (Tunisia), and linesmen Berny Ulloa Morera (Costa Rica) and Bogdan Dotschev (Bulgaria), between whom there was no common language, which wasn't ideal. Dotschev was the linesman who didn't spot Maradona's sleight of hand. Morera was later selected to run the line in the final.

1990

FLARE FAKER

The 1990 World Cup hit major controversy a year before the final stages, at the crucial qualifier between Brazil and Chile. Chile needed to win to qualify but were trailing 1-0, when in the 69th minute a flare landed near their goalkeeper, Roberto Rojas. Rojas, nicknamed 'El Cóndor' (after Chile's national symbol) for his effortless ability to 'fly' and make saves, fell to the ground in a heap holding his face. Team captain Fernando Astengo was first to 'check' on his keeper. With blood pouring down his face, Rojas and the entire Chilean team marched off the pitch and withdrew from the game, claiming their safety was at risk. The match had to be abandoned, and Chile demanded a rematch.

Strangely, while Rojas had a deep cut on his face, there were no burn marks around it, and he was evasive and contradictory in his explanations. Soon the truth came out. Rojas had had a razor blade sewn into his glove by the team's kit man. Seeing their World Cup dream slipping away, Rojas reverted to Plan B, falling to the ground and letting Astengo cut him with the hidden blade.

For his troubles, Rojas was banned from professional football for life (a punishment terminated by FIFA in 2001 when he was 43 years old), and Chile were banned from the following 1994 World Cup competition.

RIJKAARD SPITTING SHAME

The bitter rivalry between the Netherlands and neighbours West Germany turned very ugly at Italia '90. After just 22 minutes, Argentinian referee Juan Carlos Loustau had to resolve an unsavoury feud between Frank Rijkaard and Rudi Völler. It began with Rijkaard being booked for a tackle on Völler and then spitting in Völler's hair. Völler complained to the ref and, rather harshly, was booked as well.

Then, as the ball was crossed in from the following free-kick, Völler appeared to dive in search of a penalty. A furious Rijkaard twisted Völler's ear and stamped on his foot in remonstration, and Lousteau sent both players off. As the two players trudged off the pitch, Rijkaard again spat in Völler's hair.

Rijkaard later apologised to Völler for his filthy behaviour.

1) You've terminated the match prematurely, and there's no going back. Since 2005, Law 5 has stated: 'The referee may only change a decision . . . provided that he has not restarted play or terminated the match.' So you cannot now order a retake – you have to make it clear that the game is over, and later report what happened to the appropriate authority. This sort of scenario proves how important it is for officials to operate as a team.

2) No – allow the kick to go ahead. The ball is overlapping the arc, so the positioning is valid. The ball's contact with the ground can be up to 4.5 inches from the corner arc, with the ball overlapping but not actually touching the line (because the radius of a ball is 4.3 to 4.46 inches).

3) Calm the situation down, then deal with the offences in the order in which they occurred. First, award a penalty; second, dismiss the defender for the denial of an obvious goalscoring opportunity (known as DOGSO); and third, dismiss the striker for violent conduct. The fact that you hadn't blown your whistle before the punch does not change how you handle the original DOGSO incident.

▲▲ A keeper makes a stunning save from a penalty in added time. As the ball bounces behind to safety you blow for full-time – but as you do so, you see your assistant flagging wildly. He says the keeper moved off his line. What now?

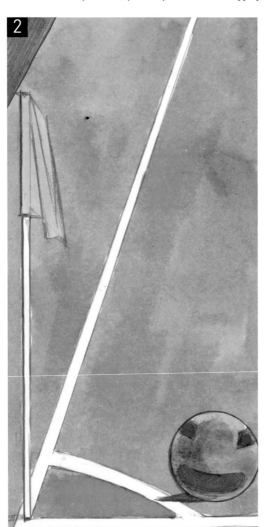

▲▲ A defender hauls a striker down in the box, denying an obvious goalscoring opportunity. But before you blow your whistle, the striker swings around and punches the defender in the face. What now? How do you restart?

◄◄ Before a corner is taken your assistant flags to tell you that the player has placed the ball outside the quadrant. You have a look, and see a small fraction of the ball still overlaps the arc. Do you intervene?

1

▲▲ You are about to blow for full-time - but the ball suddenly hits your arm and your whistle flies out of your mouth. A striker fires the deflected ball straight into the net. What now?

2

▲▲ In a match being played behind closed doors, a striker celebrates a goal by taking off his shirt. But as you run over to book him, he points out that there's no crowd, so he's not guilty of incitement. How do you proceed?

3

▲▲ A defender breaks from the wall just before a free-kick is taken on the edge of the area. The ball hits his shoulder – but before you whistle, you see it deflect up and over the keeper into the net. What now?

ANSWERS

1) Disallow the goal and indicate that the game has ended. The Laws make clear that you are the sole timekeeper, and you have decided that the game has ended – your failure to blow the whistle is irrelevant. But to avoid such a messy finish to a match, you should have reacted faster and blown your back-up whistle: all referees are advised to carry two.

2) Caution him. The law is clear: a referee must caution a player who removes his shirt, or covers his head with his shirt. Yes, there's no crowd – but the gesture could also incite opponents, and the Laws must always be applied consistently and fairly. The player can't pick and choose which count on any given day.

3) Caution him for failing to stay the required 9.15 metres distance from the ball, and award the goal. If the ball hadn't looped into the net, you would have given a retaken free-kick – keeping the advantage with the attacking side.

▲▲ In the dying moments of a cup tie, the losing side's goalkeeper goes up for a corner. But he elbows an opponent – so you send him off. His side, who have used all their subs, now want to play out the final seconds without a keeper, and focus on scoring an equaliser. Do you let them?

▲▲ Late in a brutal local derby, with the red team down to eight men after three dismissals, an opposition forward races between their two centre-backs. He's set to go clean through on goal – but simultaneously both defenders foul him in a classic sandwich manoeuvre. What happens next?

◄◄ A defender blasts the ball towards the touchline – but before it fully crosses the line it hits your assistant. As he staggers, the ball rebounds into play, allowing a striker to smack it into the net. What do you do?

▲▲ With the ball in play, an angry manager kicks a water bottle. It flies into the air and, to the manager's horror, hits an opposition player in the eye. The player can't continue, and his side have used all their subs. There's an uproar. What do you do?

▶▶ A player is subbed. Just after he steps over the touchline, and as his replacement puts one foot on to the field of play, the subbed player turns and aims a volley of foul abuse at you. What now?

▲▲ A striker is through on goal and bursts into the area – but when he feels a chasing defender grab his shirt he stops, turns and screams for a penalty and red card. You haven't yet blown your whistle. What now?

ANSWERS

1) You need to get a grip on the situation and act decisively. Send the manager from the technical area, and inform him that he will be reported to the authorities. Explain to the other manager that, unfortunately, he will now have to continue with one player fewer – and restart with a dropped ball.

2) The substitution is technically complete, so show the abusive player a red card and make sure he leaves the technical area completely. The substitute, though, can now stay on the field. This is a rare case of a red card punishing a player, but not his team – they continue with 11 men on the field, and their full remaining quota of substitutions. Restart play in the normal way.

3) If you are satisfied that the tug on the shirt represented the denial of an obvious goalscoring opportunity then send the defender off, and restart with a penalty. But you should not let the striker get away with his behaviour either – show him a yellow card for unsporting behaviour, and make it clear you don't need his input on refereeing the game.

1) As tempting as it might be to award an own goal in these circumstances, the law around penalties is clear: the kick-taker must be identified, so only that player can restart play. You should have the penalty retaken, and show the defender a yellow card. You also need to have a firm word with his captain about the team's wider dissent.

2) Show the striker a red card and quickly calm everything down. The away team can now replace the dismissed striker with one of their named substitutes and start the game with 11 players, but that substitute cannot be replaced on the bench. The change does not count as one of their three substitutions for the match. If you'd known in advance about the troubled history between the two players you could have had a quiet word with both of them before entering the field of play.

3) Yes – this is a tough call, but you shouldn't treat the goalkeeper differently to any other player who is injured. The only circumstances under which I would stop the game immediately would be if the keeper had a head injury.

▲▲ The away side are enraged by your penalty decision against them – they say you're trying to help the home side win. After calming them down, you signal for the kick to be taken, only to see the defender you penalised run in and blast the ball into his own net in protest. He turns and screams: 'Happy now?' What do you do?

▲▲ There's bad blood between a home defender and an opposition striker. During the pre-match handshake, you're stunned to see the striker punch his rival in the face. What happens now?

▲▲ A goalkeeper makes a great save – but appears to have injured his leg. As he lies prone and unable to defend his goal, a striker taps in the rebound. Do you award the goal?

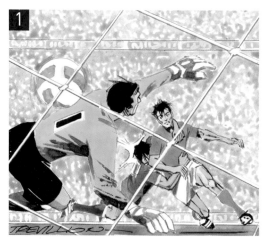

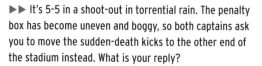
▲▲ A forward races in on goal past the last defender, who tries to drag him down with a rugby tackle. The forward wriggles clear and smashes the ball into the net – but as he does so he swings an elbow, hitting the defender in the face. Is it a penalty, a goal, or a free-kick to the defending side? Who gets sent off?

▶▶ It's 5-5 in a shoot-out in torrential rain. The penalty box has become uneven and boggy, so both captains ask you to move the sudden-death kicks to the other end of the stadium instead. What is your reply?

▲▲ The away team grab a shock winner. The scorer, already on a yellow card, celebrates by pulling down his shorts and doing a handstand. He's wearing club-coloured underwear. What action do you take?

1) First, disallow the goal and dismiss the attacking player for violent conduct: lashing out with his elbow clearly endangers the safety of his opponent. Second, caution the defender for his act of unsporting behaviour in attempting a rugby tackle. And third, award a penalty: the rugby tackle was the first offence.

2) You can agree to their request. There is a precedent: a shoot-out in a 2004 Asian Cup quarter-final – Japan v Jordan – was moved to the other end due to the state of the pitch, when the score was 0-1 after three kicks. Japan won 4-3. The only check you need to make before moving a shoot-out after it has started is to talk to stadium security, who may have asked for it to take place at a specific end for safety reasons.

3) The laws about crowd incitement don't just cover the removal of a shirt - this is exactly the same sort of gesture, so you must show him a second yellow card for unsporting behaviour, followed by a red. Restart play with a kick-off in the normal way.

ANSWERS

1) The Laws of the Game state that if, in the opinion of the referee, the feinting to confuse the goalkeeper is considered to be unsporting behaviour, the player must be cautioned. In this situation the action is clearly unsporting. Record the kick as a miss and show the kicker a yellow card.

2) It's a save – there is no retake. Players need to be able to handle distractions in a noisy stadium environment. But you should tell the ground's safety manager to tighten security around the goal area, and ask for an announcement to be made to fans. Afterwards, report what happened to the authorities.

3) Allow him to go ahead. There is nothing in the Laws to stop a manager making a decision like this, as long as the names of the two players are on the team sheet. When the players arrive and are ready to come on, they will need to wait for your signal in the usual way.

1

▲▲ It's sudden death in a penalty shoot-out. You whistle for a kick to be taken and the taker bends over as if to respot the ball. But, as he does so, in one clear movement he powerfully toe-pokes the ball forward past a bewildered stationary keeper. There's an uproar. What now?

2

▲▲ Just as a striker runs in to take a penalty, a fan lets off a firecracker behind the goal. The keeper pulls off a world-class save – but the furious striker demands a retake. The keeper is equally furious, saying the bang distracted him just as much. What do you do?

3

▶▶ Before kick-off in a non-league game, the flustered home manager says two first-choice players are stuck in traffic. He wants to keep his three subs on the bench, start with nine men and allow the latecomers to join the game when they arrive. What do you do?

1

▲▲ A penalty-taker decides on a long run-up, starting outside the D. So two defenders decide to stand just outside the D as well, between him and the ball. The taker is furious and demands you move them – but the defenders insist they're doing nothing wrong. What now?

2

HOME CHANGING ROOM

▲▲ It's a Champions League knockout game. At half-time, with the home side 3-0 down, their manager tells you his squad have been hit by food poisoning. He says over half his team are now on the toilet and he can't get seven players out for the second half. You suspect he's trying to get the game abandoned and then replayed. What do you do?

3

▲▲ A defender is deliberately tripped inside his penalty area by a striker. It is a clear foul – but before you blow your whistle, the defender picks the ball up ready to take the free-kick. Opponents scream for a penalty. What do you do?

ANSWERS

1) The defenders are right: they can stand where they want within the requirements of the penalty-kick law. If the taker wants an unusually long run-up that's fine, but he'll have to avoid the defenders on the way to the ball. If, though, one of the defenders moves to deter the kicker, book him for unsporting behaviour.

2) You cannot base your judgments on hunches or suspicions. So, after liaising with the UEFA match delegate and informing stadium security, abandon the game – a match cannot restart with fewer than seven players. You must then file a full report to UEFA, who will decide on whether to order a replay, whether the score stands, or some other outcome.

3) Every school player is told to 'play to the whistle' – the defender would have been sensible to remember that. But in this case he has got away with pre-empting your whistle: you must award a direct free-kick to the defender for the first offence – the trip by the striker.

1) Show the captain the yellow card for unsporting behaviour, and make it very clear to him that players cannot pick and choose who referees their games. He must respect you and your colleagues. The result of the coin toss stands, so he can still choose which end to attack in the first half.

2) No goal. It's a save. Blow your whistle and signal for the end of the match: the away team have won. It would have been a goal if the ball had ended its course in the net after it had touched the keeper and rebounded in, but here the ball ended its course safely in the keeper's hands. When things have calmed down, though, you should speak to the keeper, and make it clear his actions were not wise.

3) Since the substitution has been completed and play has restarted, you cannot reverse it. Send the manager to the stands for his outburst. After the game, report everything that has happened to the authorities: the fourth official will also submit a report. The matter is an issue which the club will have to deal with after the game. The substitution procedure must be monitored closely: at professional level the official substitution forms must be signed off by the manager/coach, and must be carefully checked.

▲▲ You have history with the home side and, when you call the captains together before kick-off, the home captain wins the toss but refuses to make eye contact and won't shake hands. When you question him over it, he angrily blasts the ball into the stand. What now?

▲▲ A shoot-out goes to sudden death. The away keeper has been taking constant abuse from the home fans behind the net, but holds his nerve and makes a winning save. He holds the shot, and in the same movement, roars and triumphantly hurls the ball at the fans behind him. It flies into the net. Goal or no goal?

▲▲ Just before the second half, with the home manager still in the dressing room, one of the home substitutes hands the fourth official a substitution form, apparently signed by the manager, requesting he is brought on. You sanction it – but seconds after kick-off, the furious manager appears, shouting that his signature was faked. He demands the substitution is reversed. What do you do?

1

▲▲ The home captain is injured near the end of extra time, but with all their subs used, he decides to stay on and do his best. The game goes to penalties, and reaches 10-10. The captain can hardly walk, but insists on taking his kick by putting an arm around a colleague to support himself. The opposition protest. What do you do?

2

▲▲ During a high-tension game a fan throws a paper dart made from the programme cover into the six-yard box as the players wait for a corner-kick. The goalkeeper and players nearby react, thinking it was a bottle – and during the distraction the ball is whipped in and headed into the net. What do you do?

3

▲▲ Before taking a long throw, the player wipes the ball in the wet mud by the touchline. He then uses a towel to clean just one half to give the ball 'cricketer's spin'. The opposition protest but the thrower says there's nothing in the rules to define how to clean the ball. Do you intervene?

ANSWERS

1) The player must take the kick without any help. He should have known that if he was on the field at the end of extra time then he'd be called on to take a kick – and you should have made it clear to him before the final whistle that there was a chance this would happen. Preventative refereeing makes life a lot easier. Some referees would say a player should know the Laws and so it's up to him, but I'd certainly have had a quiet word.

2) It's a tough call. If you think the distraction is minimal, allow the goal, then ask for additional stewarding behind the net. But if you think the goal was a direct result of the distraction, disallow it and restart with a dropped ball. After the game, report what happened to the authorities. It reminds me of a game I once refereed in Toronto in the North American Soccer League. I returned to the field after half-time to see the astro turf covered in paper planes. There'd been a competition to see which plane went the furthest, and because it was wet the surface was turning into papier-mache. I had to delay the restart.

3) Yes. It may not be in the Laws, but it's a clear attempt to gain an unfair advantage. Stop the throw and, only if both sides have the use of a towel, allow the player to clean and dry the whole of the ball.

FRANCE

World Cup winners	1	(1998)
World Cup runners-up	1	(2006)
Third place	2	(1958, 1986)
Fourth place	1	(1982)
World Cup hosts	1	(1998)

Michel Platini

One of the greatest playmakers in the history of football, the French midfield maestro suffered two consecutive semi-final defeats by West Germany on the game's greatest stage, in 1982 and 1986.

Zinedine Zidane

His World Cup career ended ignominiously with that infamous headbutt to earn a red card in France's 2006 World Cup final defeat, but Zidane had already been awarded the Golden Ball as player of that tournament. And his two goals in the 3–0 1998 World Cup final win over Brazil at the Stade de France meant French fans were quick to forgive their greatest-ever player's split-second loss of control.

1994

PUHL FIRST

The 1994 World Cup in the USA saw a repeat of the 1970 final between Brazil and Italy. The game at the Rose Bowl in Pasadena was refereed by the Hungarian Sándor Puhl, and was the first-ever penalty shoot-out in a World Cup final. After a goalless 120 minutes, Brazil won 3–2 on penalties after Roberto Baggio skied Italy's last kick over the crossbar.

1998

ESSE GOES WITH THE FLO

An American referee by the name of Esfandiar 'Esse' Baharmast briefly gained notoriety at the 1998 World Cup in France, when he awarded an 88th-minute penalty to Norway against Brazil in a first-round match. The score was 1-1 at the time, and the crucial decision allowed Norway to clinch a famous 2-1 win. Esse was heavily criticised initially, but the following day a TV replay from a previously unseen angle showed that Brazil defender Júnior Baiano had pulled Norway striker Tore André Flo's jersey. The ref had been spot on.

SONG DOUBLE

Cameroon's Rigobert Song earned infamy as the first player to be sent off twice in World Cup finals matches. Red-carded against Brazil in 1994, he got his marching orders in the 51st minute of Cameroon's 1-1 draw with Chile for a second bookable offence.

> Turkey's Hakan Şükür scored 11 seconds into their game against South Korea in 2002, the quickest goal in World Cup finals history.

> Brazilian striker Ronaldo scored a record 15 goals in three World Cup tournaments in 1998, 2002 and 2006.

2002

THE EYES HAVE IT

Italian referee and cult hero, Pierluigi Collina, the man with the scariest eyes in football, cemented his legacy by taking charge of the 2002 World Cup final in Yokohama. Brazil clinched their fifth World Cup, beating Germany 2-0.

POOR SHOW BY RIVALDO

Rivaldo was a star player in Brazil's 2002 World Cup triumph, but he really let himself down in a group match against Turkey. As he took up his position ready to take a corner, Hakan Ünsal kicked the ball to him, fairly hard. The ball hit him at about knee height and harmlessly bounced off the Brazilian, but he fell to the floor clutching his face. His embarrassing play-acting was hardly Oscar-worthy, but the referee was fooled, and so too was the linesman stood two yards away with a perfect view of the incident. Unsal was given a red card. The referee's actions – and FIFA's lenient punishment for 'simulation' (a fine of £5,180, but no suspension) for Rivaldo – may well have set a precedent for some of the play-acting we see today.

Pierluigi Collina was named FIFA's Best Referee of the Year six consecutive times between 1998 and 2003.

ANSWERS

1) This is one incident with two offences: handball and encroachment. First, punish the most serious, which is handball – award a direct free-kick where the handball took place. Then, show the player a yellow card for encroachment (failing to respect the required distance). You wouldn't show two yellow cards (one for deliberate handball, one for encroachment) because this is all one incident, not two.

2) No. This is a tough one. You should never have been in the way – a good referee will always try to position himself so that he avoids physical contact with players – but the player has roughly shoved you: an act of violent conduct. So you have no choice: disallow the goal and send him off. Restart with an indirect free-kick from where you were pushed.

3) During a shoot-out, the only player who can be substituted (assuming the team have substitutions remaining) is the goalkeeper. Outfield players who are injured or sent off are not replaced. So in this situation, if the two players fail to take their kicks, their penalties are recorded as misses, while the opposition continue with the shoot-out. If the opposition don't score either of these two kicks (and thus win the sudden-death shoot-out), then the kicks continue, and players can take their second penalties in any order.

▲▲ A defensive wall lines up just inside their own penalty area. As the kick is taken, you spot one of the defenders deliberately blocking the shot with his hand – but when the ball made contact, the whole wall had encroached slightly outside the box. What is your decision?

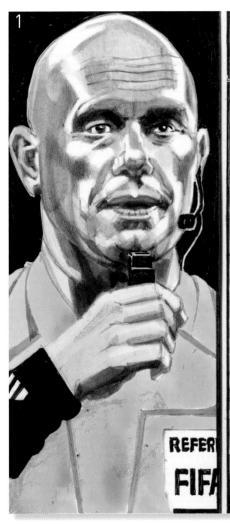

▲▲ The ball ricochets unexpectedly to a striker who is onside and who has a goalscoring opportunity. But you are in the way: he roughly shoves you out of the way and runs on to score. He then turns to apologise and pick you up while his colleagues celebrate. Do you allow the goal?

▲▲ During a sudden-death shoot-out, the away side's two weakest kick-takers have gone down, writhing around and claiming they have hamstring injuries. Their manager says they can't take their kicks, so now his two first takers, penalty experts, should go again . . . What do you do?

To mark the 100th You Are the Ref to appear on the *Observer* website, Paul Trevillion drew his all-time football hero.

▲▲ A player is furious to see he is being subbed, and screams foul abuse at his own manager. You rush over and show him a red card, but then notice the fourth official correcting the number board: he had signalled for the wrong player to come off. What do you do?

▲▲ In the second half of a relegation six-pointer, the flamboyant owner of the home side suddenly appears near the touchline and unleashes a stream of offensive, abusive language towards you. You ask him to go and sit in the stands, but he refuses, saying he owns the ground and can stand where he likes. What do you do?

▲▲ A player is off the field for treatment. He and his physio have been frantically waving for permission for him to come back on. You realise you have kept the player waiting too long, but as you prepare to wave him on, the ball breaks his way, which would put him in an onside position with a clear run on goal. What now?

ANSWERS

1) The red card stands. No player can scream obscenities during a game, whatever the provocation – including if it was a mistake by you or your colleagues. Of course, it's an error which should never have happened: clarity of signals and communication between officials and players is vital in any game.

2) He may own the ground, but he's not in charge of what takes place on and around the field of play during a match. If he refuses to return to the stands, ask security to remove him, and if that fails, tell him clearly that if he continues to refuse, the game will be abandoned. Either way, after the match send a full report to the authorities, so they can take appropriate action.

3) Delay his re-entry again. Wait for the attacking move to pass. The advice to referees is clear on this: don't call a player back on straight into an attack. But it's certainly a tricky area of the Laws. I'm not a fan of making players who are receiving treatment leave the field because of the range of problems it can cause.

ANSWERS

1) It clearly wasn't a deliberate assault, but it still represents an irresponsible, violent act, and one you need to punish. Show him a red card, have your assistant replaced by the fourth official, and restart with a kick-off as normal. Include all the details in your post-match report.

2) Your priority here is to make sure the game is played to completion if at all possible. Ask the manager to nominate one of his 10 outfield players to go in goal. Only if they refuse would you need to abandon, as the game cannot continue without a keeper. In those circumstances, you would need to take the players off the pitch, inform the stadium safety officer and police that you intend to abandon and, when they have their staff in place, confirm the abandonment. Again, pass all the details on to the authorities, who will want to take firm action.

3) Blowing up quickly to prevent a clash is valid – preventative refereeing is always a good approach when possible. With play stopped, quickly double check the ball's position. If it was fully over the line, as seems likely, award the goal. If not, check it is undamaged and restart with a dropped ball on the goal area line, parallel to the goalline.

▲▲ A player scores directly from a corner and launches into a wild celebration, kicking the flagpost out of the ground – and accidentally into your assistant's face. Your colleague is hurt and cannot continue. What now?

▲▲ A fan runs on and punches the away side's goalkeeper, badly injuring him. The keeper's manager, whose side are losing 3-0, has used all his subs, and demands you abandon the game. What now?

▲▲ A blistering volley somehow wedges in the stanchion of the goalpost – and you cannot be certain it is fully over the goalline. As players from both sides scramble towards it you blow your whistle to stop a potential confrontation. What now?

1

▲▲ After a goalmouth scramble, a striker tumbles into the net, and ends up lying face down, half on and half off the pitch, on top of the goalline. The ball is cleared and the defence move up – only for a shot to be fired back in. The keeper is beaten – but the ball clips the striker's heel before it goes in. What do you give?

2

▲▲ At half-time in a Champions League qualifier you are approached by two men offering you a bribe to 'go easy' on the away side. You saw them approach your assistant earlier, before the first half kicked-off, and now you have your doubts about some of his offside calls. What do you do?

3

▲▲ Two strikers break clear of the defensive line and are one-on-one with the keeper. The striker with the ball draws the keeper towards him, then knocks the ball sideways for his colleague to run onto and score. The keeper appeals wildly for offside. What do you award?

ANSWERS

1) Disallow the goal. The fact that the striker is face down in the mud, half off the field of play, does not mean he can't be in an 'active' position. The ball has hit him on the way in, so you must declare him offside.

2) If you have lost confidence in your assistant, and you believe his decisions to be suspicious, you must arrange to have him removed from the second half, with the fourth official taking over the role. And with any illegal approach, or any suspicion of an illegal approach, you must immediately report what has happened to the UEFA match delegate at the game. Fortunately the chances of this happening in the Champions League are slim due to the high security around players and officials: no one is allowed in the tunnel area without the appropriate accreditation.

3) It's a goal. The keeper would have a point if the second striker had been ahead of the first when the ball was passed, and had to go back for the ball. But here the colleague is not in an offside position as he was behind the ball when it was knocked sideways.

1) With a head injury the decision is simple – even if you suspect the player may have gone to ground deliberately to break up play, the priority has to be ensuring medical attention is provided immediately. So stop play, allow for treatment, then restart the game with a free-kick for the offence from which advantage was played. It's tough on the attacking side, but safety is paramount. You should monitor the medical treatment so that you are satisfied the injury is genuine: if you have a suspicion that the player faked the injury, then you can show him a yellow card for simulation (unsporting behaviour).

2) It's a goal: the ball has made contact with an outfield player before going into the net. Show the defender a yellow card for deliberate handball. You would not show him a red for denying a goal with his hand because a goal cannot be scored directly from a throw-in.

3) Offside. Your assistant is correct to hesitate: he is using the 'wait and see' technique to judge whether the striker becomes active. In this instance the deflection does not play him onside. 'Played on' was taken out of the Laws in 1978.

▲▲ A striker is fouled as he runs towards goal, but he retains possession so you play advantage. However, as he runs you notice an opposition player has gone down, apparently in agony, clutching his head. What do you do – and how does play restart?

▲▲ A player hurls a giant long throw into the box. It eludes the goalkeeper and everyone else and is flying into the net when a defender instinctively tries to punch it round the post to safety. He only succeeds in punching it into the net. What action do you take?

▲▲ A midfielder slips a beautiful ball towards a striker who was standing in an offside position. A defender stretches to intercept and gets a slight touch on the ball before it reaches the striker. Your assistant hesitates. What do you do?

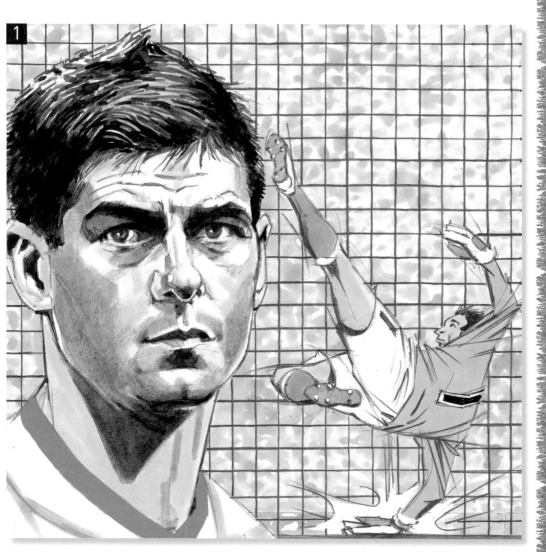

1

1) The game does not start with your whistle - the ball must be kicked and move forward - so there is still time to make the change. Allow the manager to bring on another player to play in goal: either a goalkeeper from the named substitutes or, if there is no reserve keeper on the bench, a registered keeper from outside the match-day squad. If he does use a keeper from the bench, the team can add another substitute to replace him.

▲▲ You blow your whistle for kick-off at the start of a game, but the player hesitates – he's spotted his keeper lying injured. It looks like the keeper fell badly while dangling from his crossbar – and his manager now wants to replace him, without using up a substitution. What do you do?

2

3

2) First, restore order, then make a decision about the striker's mockery: is it really unsporting behaviour? It's a tough call, but in these circumstances I would award the goal and have a quiet word. Only if the striker had continued mocking the keeper, or provoked the other players further, would I show a second yellow. Also, be ready to caution for dissent any opponent who continues his protest.

3) It was a tough one to read but you made a decision. Even if you think you were deceived by the nasty red mark, it is best to stand by your call. Have the penalty taken – then detail everything, including the physio's remark, in your report. All in all, not the tidiest piece of refereeing.

▲▲ A striker, on a yellow card after a clash with the goalkeeper, breaks through on goal. As he rounds the keeper he decides to take revenge and mock his rival - kneeling down and nodding the ball into the net. Opponents want him sent off for unsporting behaviour. What now?

▲▲ A striker falls as he beats the last defender in the box. You blow for a penalty and send the defender off. You had been unsure if it was a foul or a dive but are convinced it was a foul when you see a nasty mark on the striker's leg. Then you overhear the physio saying it is an old wound. The doubt in your mind returns. What now?

▲▲ You give permission for an indirect free-kick to be taken quickly. The keeper, furious with your original decision, is still walking back towards his goal after protesting – so the kick-taker deliberately aims the ball towards him. It clips the keeper's shoulder and goes in. Is it a goal?

▲▲ A bald player whose first language is not English returns to the pitch for the second half with words written on his head in his native language – and in indelible ink. The player claims it means 'Come on United'. But the away captain says it's an abusive message aimed at you. What now?

▲▲ The home team's keeper goes off injured – and with no subs left, they put a tall striker in goal. They then win a corner and notify you they are changing their keeper again, so the tall striker can go upfield. The corner comes to nothing, and they swap back. They then win another corner, and ask to swap again. The away team are furious. What do you do?

1

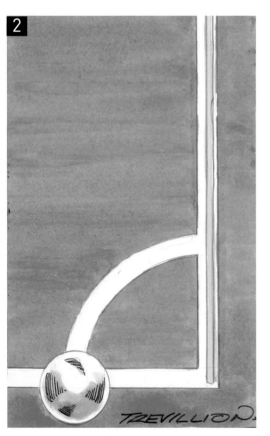

▲▲ A striker races clear into the area but is clipped from behind, resulting in his boot coming off. But he keeps his balance and manages to get his shot away – smacking the ball into the net with his socked foot. Goal or no goal?

2

3

▲▲ A corner-taker places the ball largely outside the corner quadrant, with most of it off the field of play. Opponents shout, and their fans behind the goalline are screaming abuse at you. What now?

▲▲ A player has treatment for a cut to his head, which has left his white shirt soaked in blood. He's fit to return – but there are no spare shirts. His manager wants him to play in his white vest instead. What now?

ANSWERS

1) Goal. Stopping play for a boot coming off is at your discretion: you would only do it if there was a clear danger to the player. The best option here is to play advantage and award the goal. And, if you consider the defender's challenge reckless, show him a yellow card for unsporting behaviour.

2) They have a point – but do they understand what 'inside' means in the Laws of the Game? If any part of the ball is overlapping the painted quadrant line, even if 99 per cent is outside the quadrant, it is considered inside. Players should know that – and officials always monitor it carefully.

3) He cannot take part – neither in a vest nor topless. He and his manager should know that players cannot take part unless their equipment conforms with the law, which has been clear on this since 2002 when Cameroon tried to compete in sleeveless vests. Sleeves are compulsory, and clubs have to make sure spare shirts are available. In this case, his team go down to 10 men.

ANSWERS

1) A terrific question. As always, think clearly, step by step. The striker was in an offside position when the shot was struck – but once the keeper gathers the ball, however quickly he then rolls it forwards, the initial phase for penalising the offside position ends. This is the keeper's error – he has effectively passed the ball to an opponent in open play. So allow the goal.

2) Attempting to trip an opponent is an offence, whether it succeeds or not. If the striker had managed to score then clearly you could have played advantage, but as it is you need to intervene. Award the penalty and, if you judge that the attempted trip clearly denied an obvious goalscoring opportunity, then issue a red card too.

3) It's a nice piece of quick thinking from the diminutive defender, but it's also an offence, so stop the game. Although he has denied a goal, you can only send a player off if he denies a goal by handling the ball. So show him a yellow card for unsporting behaviour and restart with an indirect free-kick to the attacking team, taken on the goal area line parallel to the goalline, from the point nearest the incident.

▲▲ A keeper saves a long-range shot, then instantly rolls the ball out a few yards in front of him, ready to boot it upfield. But he fails to spot that a striker, who was in an offside position when the shot was struck, is now racing towards him. The striker reaches the ball first and knocks it into the net. Is it a goal?

▲▲ As a player weaves into the box, a chasing defender tries to trip him. Although he stumbles, the forward manages to get his shot away – but it's weaker than it would have been and is easily saved. He demands a penalty. What now?

▲▲ A 5ft 4in full-back, guarding the post for a corner, leaps to block a goal-bound header. As he nods the ball clear, you notice he has boosted his jump by pulling himself up on the netting. The ball remains in play. What now?

▲▲ A player smashes the decisive kick of a penalty shoot-out against the bar – but it rebounds out, hits the keeper and goes into the net. Both sides celebrate. Who has won?

▲▲ Your assistant has made several tight calls against the away side – prompting one of their subs to take revenge. As the assistant sprints along the line to keep up with the home side's winger, the sub rolls a water bottle into his path. He goes flying, while the winger goes on to score. What now?

▲▲ The away side's player-manager is having a shocker in midfield. But when, in the second half, his assistant signals for him to come off, he refuses to leave the pitch: he says he's overruling the substitution, and wants the game to restart. What now?

1) In the past this would have counted as a miss, which is why this sort of situation still causes confusion – but the law has changed. Now you must wait until the ball has completed its path before either awarding a goal, or ruling the kick has been missed or saved. In this case, the deflection is a valid one, and the goal stands. It's very rare that this sort of thing happens, but it does from time to time – again proving how important it is to be aware of law changes.

2) As soon as your assistant was knocked over, you should have stopped play: the sub has clearly endangered his safety, and deserves a red card – meaning his side will continue the game with 11 men, but will have one fewer sub available. But as you did not stop the game, you should now award the goal, having effectively played advantage: there is no reason to penalise the home side, who have done nothing wrong.

3) This really isn't your call: the away side need to resolve it in a timely fashion. Ask the team's captain and the player-manager to come with you to the touchline, and urge them to find a solution in a professional, dignified way. But ultimately, if the player-manager insists he is overruling the change, that is his decision. Restart the game with him still on the field.

SPAIN

World Cup winners	1	(2010)
World Cup runners-up	-	
Third place	-	
Fourth place	1	(1950)
World Cup hosts	-	

Andrés Iniesta

Midfielder Iniesta was a star of Spain's first-ever World Cup triumph in 2010. At the heart of Spain's revolutionary 'tiki-taka' pass-and-move style of football, he scored the winning goal four minutes from the end of extra time in the final against the Netherlands, and was named man of the match.

2006

POLL'S THREE-CARD TRICK

After two excellent performances, English referee Graham Poll looked a possible candidate to take charge of the final. However, his hopes were dashed by a spectacular blunder during his third match of the tournament, between Croatia and Australia, when he showed three yellow cards to Josip Šimunić before sending him off. Poll revealed later that he had written down Šimunić's number (3) in the wrong column when booking him for the second time, so it appeared that Australian Craig Moore had been booked instead. Subsequently, Poll was not included in the referee pool for the knockout stages.

ZIZOU SHOCKER

Argentinian referee Horacio Elizondo was faced with the unenviable task of sending off football legend Zinedine 'Zizou' Zidane in his last-ever match – the 2006 World Cup final between France and Italy at the Olympic Stadium, Berlin.

Elizondo had no option but to show the red card as Zidane headbutted Italian defender Marco Materazzi during the second period of extra time. Zidane had also been sent off against Saudi Arabia in the 1998 World Cup.

VALENTIN'S CARD FRENZY

Russian referee Valentin Ivanov brandished 16 yellow cards and four red cards in a second-round match between Portugal and the Netherlands at the 2006 World Cup. The four red cards were a first for a World Cup match, taking the total number of sendings-off in the tournament to 23, breaking the previous record set in 1998.

2010

THE HAND OF HENRY

An intentional handball by Thierry Henry was decisive in France's narrow World Cup play-off victory against the Republic of Ireland in November 2009. Henry touched the ball twice with his hand before making the vital assist for William Gallas's equaliser in the second leg in Paris to clinch a 2-1 aggregate win. After this huge injustice, the Minister of Justice of Ireland requested the match to be replayed, but France took their place in the finals in South Africa.

LAMPS'S 'GOAL' AGONY

Forty-four years after Geoff Hurst and England got the benefit of a goalline decision, Frank Lampard was far less fortunate. With half-time approaching and England 2-1 down to Germany in the first round of the knockout stages, Lampard's piledriver shot smacked against the crossbar and bounced down. Unlike Hurst's shot, the ball clearly landed over the line, but Uruguayan referee Jorge Larrionda waved play on. Germany went on to win 4-1, leaving all England supporters wondering what might have been if goalline technology had been in use and Lamps's equaliser had counted.

FULL ENGLISH

Englishman Howard Webb was given the honour of refereeing the 2010 World Cup final between Spain and the Netherlands at Soccer City in Johannesburg. Webb easily broke the previous record for most cards shown in a World Cup final (six in 1986), issuing an amazing 14 yellow cards (John Heitinga was sent off for two cautionable offences). And there could have been another sending-off – Dutchman Nigel de Jong later admitted he was fortunate not to be red-carded for a high challenge, but Webb had a poor view of the incident.

ANSWERS

1) Accept the decision: it's not a goal. Hawk-Eye has been through some incredibly stringent testing, and the system wouldn't have been given the go-ahead by the Premier League if it wasn't 100 per cent foolproof. The hardware, using data from seven cameras around each goal, sends a signal to the referee, without fail, only when the ball crosses the goalline, whether in the air or on the ground. As in other sports, Hawk-Eye's decision is final and referees need to accept it, even when they have their doubts.

2) This is obviously unsporting behaviour. Caution the player for his comments and then signal for the penalty to be taken. You would not change your decision to award the kick, or to punish him for diving, based on what he whispers.

3) Stop play and award an indirect free-kick to the attacking team. The keeper is allowed to handle the ball inside his own penalty area – his only offence here is playing the ball from the back-pass. And, because the incident happened inside the six-yard box, make sure the free-kick is taken from the six-yard line parallel to the goalline.

▲▲ A shot thunders against the underside of the bar, bounces down and away from the goal. Attackers scream that it crossed the line, and you agree with them – but the Hawk-Eye system does not react. Do you overrule Hawk-Eye and award a goal, or accept its decision?

▲▲ You give a penalty after a striker goes sprawling in the box. But as the fouled player prepares to take the spot-kick, he whispers, 'I can't believe you bought that dive' and winks. What, if anything, should you do?

▲▲ A goalkeeper, already on a yellow card, dives and manages to get his hand to a badly sliced, deliberate back-pass, preventing what would have been an own goal. What action do you take?

▲▲ A striker is mobbed by teammates after scoring, and emerges from the bundle minus his shirt. You had already booked him after his first goal for removing his shirt – but this time you are not certain he did it himself. What now?

▲▲ In a lower-league game the furious home manager hurls his water bottle – accidentally hitting the away side's last remaining substitute in the eye, just as he is about to come on for an injured colleague. The sub's manager is outraged: he refuses to play with only 10 men, and demands you abandon the game instead. What do you do?

▲▲ A striker about to score is brought down by a combination of the keeper's trailing leg and a rash, reckless tackle from behind. Who do you punish, and how?

ANSWERS

1) You need to base your decisions on what you or your colleagues have observed – and in this case you did not see the player himself remove his shirt. So call him and his captain together, and inform them both, via a public rebuke, that the behaviour is unacceptable. Make it clear that if there is a repeat, whoever scored the goal will be cautioned. Restart with a kick-off.

2) Quickly control the situation. First, send the home manager from the technical area and tell him he will be reported for his actions. Second, inform the away manager that there are no grounds to abandon the game, but that the incident will be included in your report – authorities may later decide to award his side three points or order a replay. Then, with order restored, play out the remainder of the match.

3) As the two fouls occur simultaneously, you have a choice here. First signal for a penalty, then deal with the offenders. Both players are guilty of denying an obvious goalscoring opportunity, but it was only one opportunity – one goal denied – so only one player is sent off. And, as the defender's challenge was clearly reckless, while the keeper may have been unlucky, the defender is the one who merits the red card most.

1) Corner flagposts are compulsory – but you should always avoid abandonment unless absolutely necessary. So ask the groundsman to try and repair the post with tape, or even consider using a long broom handle, unless it represents a danger to players. Do not delay the game while this goes on: you can restart without a flagpost. And, even if no solution can be found, I would complete the match, reporting what happened to the authorities.

2) As the offence took place off the field, you cannot award a penalty. Caution the defender if it was a reckless foul, or send him off if it involved excessive force, endangered the opponent's safety, or if it constituted denying an obvious goalscoring opportunity. Restart with an indirect free-kick from where the ball was when play was stopped.

3) It's a goal. The corner-taker played to the whistle, but the keeper did not. Calm the situation down, and tell the pigeon-kicker to be more aware of how his actions may be perceived. Had the kick been less than gentle, though, you would have dealt with the situation differently; had it constituted violent conduct then it would have been a red-card offence.

▲▲ A player celebrates a crucial late goal by dancing around the corner flagpost – and snaps it by mistake. The groundsman tells you there are no spares. What happens now?

▲▲ A winger skips along the goalline and nutmegs a defender, stepping out of play in the process. But as he does so he is brought down – the foul taking place off the field of play. The ball rolls out to safety. What do you do?

▲▲ A player about to take a corner is distracted by a pigeon landing at his feet. He reacts by gently kicking the bird away with the side of his boot – an act that enrages the opposition keeper. As the corner is floated over, the keeper, a well-known animal lover, races out of his goal to protest – and the ball is headed into his empty net. What now?

▲▲ A striker is brought down inside the area, but the ball runs to his teammate who is facing an open goal. You delay whistling – but are surprised to see the player deliberately let the ball roll between his legs and out of play. He clearly feels a red card and a penalty is of more use to his side than a goal. What do you do?

▶▶ Before kick-off in a park game you notice that the fronts of the goalposts are an unusual triangular shape. It's the same at both ends. What do you do?

▲▲ A striker, already on a yellow, celebrates a goal by grabbing a spare ball from a ballboy and booting it into the stands. Opponents howl for a second yellow – but the striker says it wasn't the match ball, so he's done nothing wrong. What do you do?

1) You've rightly delayed to see if an advantage has accrued – the fact that the player has deliberately failed to take that opportunity should not change your thinking. There was no advantage, so award a penalty-kick. However, the player has taken a bizarre gamble: you would only show a red card to the goalkeeper if he denied the first striker an obvious goalscoring opportunity – and there was a defender on the line. Players are best advised to focus on playing, not refereeing.

2) If there is no other pitch available, and the posts cannot be changed, you cannot play the match. Goalposts and crossbars must be square, rectangular, round or elliptical in shape, and must not be dangerous to players. Report the situation to the competition secretary.

3) The player has taken a daft risk. Your decision should be based on whether he has a) delayed the restart or b) incited the crowd. If he has, it is indeed a second yellow card. But if not, issue the player with a clear public rebuke, and restart the game with a kick-off. My instinct in this case would be to stick with a firm rebuke.

ANSWERS

1) Award an indirect free-kick to the attacking team. Once the keeper has released the ball on the ground it has to be played or touched by another player before he can pick it up again. That's why goalkeepers need to be so alert to make sure opponents are well away from them before they let go of the ball like this.

2) You have two options here: stop play immediately and show the defender a yellow card for unsporting behaviour or, if the kick-taker has continued his run, await the outcome of the penalty. If the player scores, allow the goal and then caution the defender; if he misses, award a retake and, again, show the defender a yellow. It is not a red-card offence as the ball has to be in play for it to count as denying an obvious goalscoring opportunity.

3) It's not a penalty: the defenders have not committed an offence by holding hands – and neither has the forward by standing in an offside position. That only becomes an issue if he plays or touches the ball. For instance, if the ball was to rebound off the goalkeeper, post or crossbar to the attacker he will be considered to have gained an advantage and will be declared offside if he touches it. So there is no reason to intervene here: deal with the outcome of the free-kick in the usual way.

1

▲▲ A goalkeeper bounces the ball a couple of times, then rolls it out in front of him ready to clear upfield. But then he spots an attacker lurking behind him, so lunges forwards and picks the ball up again. What do you do?

2

▲▲ As a penalty-taker starts his long run-up, a defender on the edge of the D tugs his shirt. What action do you take?

3

▲▲ At a free-kick, a forward stands just behind the wall in an offside position, intending to step back onside before the kick is taken. But as the ball is kicked, the wall joins hands and traps him offside. He demands a penalty. What now?

1

2

▲▲ A defender, being treated off the pitch for a head injury, sees an opposition winger race clear of the defence. Without your permission, he sprints two yards onto the pitch and trips him up. What do you do?

▶▶ It's wet weather and the touchlines are churning up. At half-time your two assistants suggest they run the lines on the opposite quarters of the pitch instead, which are not so muddy. Do you allow it?

3

TREVILLION

▲▲ A defender passes the ball back to a teammate inside the box, but, seeing an opponent racing in, the keeper shouts for him to leave it and picks it up. What now?

ANSWERS

1) Stop play. Show the defender a yellow card for entering the field without permission. If the trip was reckless, show him a second yellow followed by a red. Restart play with a direct free-kick. It's not a straight red card for denying an obvious goalscoring opportunity because the foul was two yards from the touchline – so the goalscoring opportunity was not obvious.

2) Yes – let them switch. These days it is standard practice worldwide for assistants to run outside the right wing, to improve consistency, especially in international matches. But in my early days as a referee, linesmen would often switch at half-time to ensure they were running on a decent surface – and there's nothing in the Laws now to stop a referee making changes if the conditions demand it.

3) Allow play to continue. The law on back-passes is clear: it defines them as a ball 'deliberately kicked to the goalkeeper by a teammate'. This was not the case, so the keeper has done nothing wrong by picking the ball up.

ANSWERS

1) This is a grim situation for you to be put in, but you have to be consistent on 'outside agents' – even when it means you are effectively penalising an innocent party. So, as is always the case when the ball strikes an outside agent, stop play and restart with a dropped ball. As for the implications of your decision: you need to put your faith in the stadium security staff, and, after the game, in the authorities to react appropriately to what took place.

2) You are not a doctor: you cannot make a decision about whether or not he is faking the injury. So apply the Laws: a goalkeeper who is injured during a shoot-out can be replaced by a named substitute, provided the team has not used the maximum number of subs permitted.

3) Sadly, the two sides are not infringing any Laws: passing the ball and losing possession is all part of the game, and passing to each other does not count as time-wasting as the ball is in live play. So, however wrong it feels, let the game come to its conclusion and include everything that happened in your report. This is another one for the competition organisers to consider.

▲▲ In added time of a play-off semi-final, a striker lobs the keeper. It looks certain to be the winning goal – until an opposition fan manages to hurl a matchday programme at the ball and deflect it to safety. Do you award the goal, or disallow it and risk a riot?

▲▲ In a penalty shoot-out a young, nervous goalkeeper is having a shocker. Before the next kick he goes down, claiming injury. You think he is faking it. Do you let his manager replace him with the substitute keeper, or tell him to play on?

▲▲ Three minutes before the end of the final game of the season between two relegation contenders, word comes through that a draw will be enough to save both sides. So, with the score at 2-2, both sides stop playing, and start passing the ball to each other. What do you do?

1

▲▲ During a televised match a famously outspoken, *Guardian*-reading striker celebrates scoring by running over to an advert for a payday loans company and making a thumbs-down gesture. He has already been booked. What do you do?

▲▲ You award a last-minute penalty – only to discover that the torrential rain has completely wiped out the penalty spot. You pace out 12 yards – but both teams demand that the spot is properly measured and repainted before they will continue. What now?

▲▲ In a European tie the away side's star striker says he has been racially abused by home fans – so he walks off the pitch in disgust. You did not hear the abuse, and his manager wants to bring on a sub to replace him. What do you do?

1) There is no provision in the Laws for an outfield player to be withdrawn or replaced once penalties are under way. If the player is really physically unable to take his turn, his kick is recorded as a miss – so in this situation, as he is still upright, he may as well have a go at goal. So, with or without him, the shoot-out continues as normal.

2) It's a clear decision: delaying the restart is a cautionable offence, so issue him with a second yellow card, then a red. And, before restarting the game with the throw-in, make sure another player has gone in goal – a substitute keeper or an outfield player if all the subs have already been used. The game cannot restart without a keeper.

3) There's not much you can do about this: it's not in the Laws that he has to shake your hand, and failing to do so does not represent dissent. Keep a close eye on him during the game – he's clearly in a confrontational frame of mind, and, if he later picks up a yellow or red card in the game, you can mention what happened in your post-match report to the authorities.

TREVILLION·

▲▲ A player scores in a tense penalty shoot-out, but pulls a hamstring in the process. The shoot-out continues, and eventually reaches 18-18 – meaning it is his turn again. The opposition insist he has to take the kick as he can still walk – but the player's manager wants to withdraw him. What do you do?

▲▲ The away team's goalkeeper, who is already on a yellow card, races out to the touchline and boots the ball high into the stand. A ballboy immediately leaps up to supply a spare to the home team for a quick throw – but the keeper snatches the ball and runs back to his goal. The opposition are outraged. What now?

▲▲ At the beginning of a game, the away captain, who you sent off in a previous match, refuses to shake your outstretched hand. What action, if any, can you take?

▲▲ The home captain approaches you and says four of his players are deeply offended by an opposition sub's tattoo, which mocks their religious beliefs. They refuse to play on unless he is removed from the bench. What is your decision?

▲▲ A winger jinks into the box and goes down over a defender's leg. You blow the whistle and point to the penalty spot – but your assistant calls you over: he is adamant that the player dived. He says he is 100 per cent certain the winger cheated. What now?

▲▲ A young forward, already on a yellow card, unleashes a ferocious volley, and swears loudly in delight as it screams into the net. Opponents race over and demand a second yellow for offensive language. What now?

ANSWERS

1) You need to be ready to handle such issues with sensitivity. Ask the sub to cover up the tattoo with tape or clothing, and inform club officials and the sub himself after the game that you intend to report the matter to the authorities. Rules banning players displaying 'religious statements' are in place for good reason. The club and the individual can expect to face sanctions.

2) How much faith do you have in what you saw? You can change your decision as long as play has not restarted. Talk to your assistant – if you are convinced you are correct, proceed with the penalty; otherwise, caution the winger for simulation and restart with an indirect free-kick to the defending team.

3) First, you are the ref: if any of the opponents take their protests too far, consider cautioning one or more of them. As for the forward: while I don't condone bad language, you need to show some common sense. Award the goal, and have a firm word with player and captain. Only if the player used seriously offensive language would you need to take it further: that could be punished by a straight red card. Clearly, though, it is best to avoid that if possible.

▲▲ A penalty-taker slips as he strikes the ball, and ends up just nudging it forward. As players race in from outside the area to reach it, a teammate gets there first and smashes it home. Goal, or something else?

▲▲ A striker, through on goal, is clearly clipped by the last man. He manages to stay upright for one stride, but then sprawls theatrically, and appeals for a red card. What do you do?

▲▲ A forward makes a fair shoulder charge on a keeper who has both hands on the ball, but also has both feet off the ground. The keeper loses possession and the ball drops into the net. What now?

THE ARTIST: Paul Trevillion

Born and raised in Tottenham, north London, Paul Trevillion could not read or write until he was thirteen – but his artistic talent enabled him to produce artwork for *The Eagle* while he was still at school. From the 1960s to the 1980s, Trevillion's art featured in almost every national newspaper in Britain. Famous for illustrating such classic series as Roy of the Rovers, he also illustrated the Gary Player Golf Class, which appeared in over 1,000 newspapers worldwide. Paul has met and drawn some of sport's biggest names, including Pelé, Bobby Moore, George Best, Franz Beckenbauer, Jack Nicklaus, Tiger Woods, Sugar Ray Robinson and Michael Jordan.

Away from his art, Paul has enjoyed a full and varied life, with highlights including a stand-up career supporting the likes of Tommy Cooper and Norman Wisdom, being crowned world speed-kissing champion, inventing a split-handed golf putting technique, and having coffee with – then drawing – Winston Churchill.

Trevillion's cult classic football strip, You Are the Ref, has appeared weekly in the *Observer* since 2006 and became a permanent interactive exhibit at the National Football Museum in Manchester in 2012.

THE REFEREE: Keith Hackett

The voice of You Are the Ref since 1981, Keith Hackett has been synonymous with refereeing for decades: first as one of England's top officials, and then as general manager of the Professional Game Match Officials Limited – the body in charge of the nation's referees. He is counted amongst the top 100 referees of all time in a list maintained by the International Federation of Football History and Statistics.

Keith started refereeing in local leagues in the Sheffield area as a teenager in 1960, and became a Football League referee in 1976. He became one of the youngest-ever Cup Final referees when he presided over the 1981 match between Spurs and Manchester City at Wembley, as well as the replay. Five years later he refereed the 1986 League Cup final, and he also officiated at Euro '88 and that year's Olympic Games at Seoul. He retired from refereeing just short of his fiftieth birthday in 1994.